Island Between

UNIVERSITY OF ALASKA PRESS
Fairbanks, 1977

Exclusive Distributor:
ISBS, Inc.
P. O. Box 555
Forest Grove, OR 97116

Island Between

MARGARET E. MURIE

IN TRIBUTE

to a tireless researcher who loved the Eskimo people,
this book is dedicated to the memory of

OTTO WM. GEIST

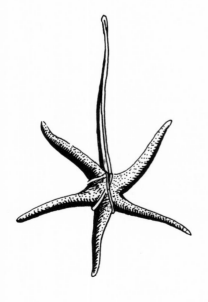

PREFACE

THE PRESIDENT of the University of Alaska through its first thirty years was an educator with a hobby and that hobby was Arctic archeology. When, in 1926, Dr. Charles E. Bunnell and Otto Wm. Geist met, the St. Lawrence Island archeological investigations of the University of Alaska had their beginning.

For the greater part of eight years Otto Geist lived on St. Lawrence Island with the Eskimos, in Eskimo houses, ate Eskimo food, wore Eskimo clothes, went hunting and trapping and fishing with the Eskimos, was adopted into a family, given the name "Aghvook" the whale, sacred above all animals, and was allowed to participate in ceremonies, funerals, and sacrifices, a privilege rarely granted a white person. On his left wrist was tattooed the image of Aghvook, and he looked on the island as home and its people as his people.

In the course of these years of strenuous work in excavations[1] there grew also in Otto's notebooks a wealth of material on the history of the big island, on the legends, ceremonies, beliefs and notable incidents in the lives of its people.

With these notes as source material, with constant help from Dr. Geist and constant encouragement from Dr. Bunnell, this book was written. In the course of the work I had also, through Dr. Bunnell's thoughtfulness, the opportunity to spend several weeks on the Island with its people, an adventure which has enriched my life ever since.

The Eskimo words and names used in this book are in the language of St. Lawrence Island and may differ slightly from those of other Eskimo localities. The stories used in the course of the narrative are quoted verbatim as written for Dr. Geist by Silook, one of the islanders who went further with the government school teachers than most of them did at that time. In fact, he told me himself: "I am a literary man."

So far as we are able to know, from archeology, recorded history, recent customs, and the personal testimony of the Island's people, collected in Dr. Geist's notebooks, every fact, every incident, is true and actually happened at some time in the Island's history. I have merely woven all into a narrative. I have tried to write from the Eskimo point of view, and to keep the whole story as straight and unpretentious and natural as are the people themselves. My aim has been to present a complete picture of life as it was lived in an Eskimo community before it was touched and altered by the arrival of white men.

Birds and animals mentioned in the story were identified by my husband Olaus J. Murie, and the drawings were done by him also. Plants were identified from specimens I collected on the island by Dr. Louis O. Williams of the Chicago Museum of Natural History; the mushrooms by Dr. D. H. Linder of the Farlow Herbarium, and the marine forms by Miss F. LaMont and Dr. Willard G. Van Name of the American Museum of Natural History. To Dr. Leslie A. Marchand, professor of English at the University of Alaska in its early days and later at Rutgers University, I am grateful for many good suggestions.

Above all I am keenly conscious of the fact that the great collection of data on the intimate life of the Island's people is the product of the foresight and enthusiasm of Dr. Bunnell plus the zeal and pioneering field work of Dr. Geist, and that it was their aid and encouragement which made the writing possible.

And now it is my hope that the people of St. Lawrence Island today will find this story harmonious with their knowledge, their feelings, their memories, and their love of their island.

CONTENTS

PREFACE   vii
AN INTRODUCTION: AHIPANI, *In the Back Ages*   1
THE SETTING: *Time, Place, People*   10

PART ONE: *Being, Moon by Moon, a Year on Sevuokuk*

KANAHYUNGASI: *Moon of Frost Forming Under the Roof*
CHAPTER I   Coming of Siko   17

KAHLOOVIK: *Moon of Getting Tom-Cod with the Throwing Net*
CHAPTER II   Siko and Iviek   23
CHAPTER III   Ahrolah, The Dance   31
CHAPTER IV   For a Wife   37
CHAPTER V   The Singer   41

NAHZEGHOHSEK: *Moon of Approaching of Young Seal*
CHAPTER VI   Winter Festival   47
CHAPTER VII   Magic Lamp Bowl   59

TAHEGLOKHSEK: *Moon of Appearing of Mukluk, Young Big Seal*
CHAPTER VIII   Toozak and Kaka   65

HOGHVEK: *Moon for Using Bird Slings*
CHAPTER IX   Toozak the Trapper   71
CHAPTER X   Iviek Again   77
CHAPTER XI   Aghvook is Coming   87

KEGUMAHNA: *Summer-Woman Moon*
CHAPTER XII   Aghvook Comes   95
CHAPTER XIII   Baleen and Munktuk   101

PENAHVEK: *Moon When Rivers Begin to Flow*
CHAPTER XIV   The Sorcerer Dreams   107
CHAPTER XV   Toozak Runs   113

ANGOTAHVEK: *Moon of Plant Gathering*

CHAPTER XVI   On the Mountain   121

PALEHVEK: *Moon of Plants Withering*

CHAPTER XVII   Ungiakpuk   129

AKOMAK: *Moon of Sitting*

CHAPTER XVIII   In the Storm   137
CHAPTER XIX   Those Two   145

PART TWO: *Being the Later Years*

CHAPTER XX   Son of Toozak   151
CHAPTER XXI   To the Lagoon   157
CHAPTER XXII   The Best Spirit World   163
CHAPTER XXIII   After the Storm   171
CHAPTER XIV   Siko Again   179
CHAPTER XXV   With the South Wind   187
CHAPTER XXVI   Their Story   195
CHAPTER XXVII   Ungiakpuk Again   199
CHAPTER XXVIII   The Year 1878   205
CHAPTER XXIX   Return to Kukulik   215
CHAPTER XXX   End and Beginning   217

NOTES   223

GLOSSARY   225
The Characters
The Moons
And the Other Words

·AHIPANI·
In The Back Ages

AGES AND AGES AGO, the Eskimo people say, a great giant lived in the far north. One day he happened to be standing with one foot on the Siberian coast and the other on the shores of Alaska. The two continents are not very far apart there, so the giant stood comfortably, looking out over the world.

As it happened, he chanced to look down at the narrow strip of water between his feet, and nonchalantly reached down and took up a handful of the sand and stone of the ocean's bed. He stood looking at it and idly squeezing the water from it. Then he raised his great arm and threw the handful of dirt and rock out before him into the water. It stayed there—an island between the two continents.

Many centuries later the island was found by White Men and named St. Lawrence, because they sighted it on that Saint's day, August 8, 1728. But to the island's own Inuit (The People) it is still "Sevuokuk," meaning, literally, "squeezed."

The casually created island lay there and received the long, long procession of life up over its shores. There was even an age when warmer winds swept over it, when the ice was unknown, and when the island bore trees, forests of the Sequoia.

Then the top of the world grew cold again and things changed. Yet Life was there, and grew and spread, abundantly, perhaps not as richly as in southern parts, but strongly, tenaciously adapting itself to the cold, strong climate of this part of the world.

The geologists say that for part of this long-gone time there was land all the way across at some point between the two continents. Over this land bridge passed bears, mountian sheep, and even lions to find new environ-

1

ments, some to develop new species, all the way up and down the vast continent to the east.

In this complex array of animal groups, man appeared, in western regions. Recently, as we count geologic time, and humbly at first, he was looking out upon a hostile world with wonder and fear, competing with creatures much stronger than himself, living by his wits, suffering much, but surviving. And he, too, had the Wanderlust. From the old world he kept pushing across Asia eastward, and it was natural that he too should find and use the land between the continents and travel on east and south and become the Indian of North and South America.

Then came the centuries of sinking of the land, of ocean flowing over it, so that the first men of Eskimo stock to reach the Siberian coast looked across miles of inhospitable sea to the faint shadow of another land floating there on the horizon, tantalizing, tempting, and that land was the island Sevuokuk.

So there must have come a day when courage and curiosity welled up tremendously in the souls of some of these people; they had learned to make boats, and they began to think of great journeying.

· · · · ·

On a rocky beach below high tawny cliffs, brown-skinned, fur-clad people are launching a long skin-boat into blue water just lately freed from its winter cover of ice.

A great shout and the boat is shoved in and the whole group moves quickly back and forth, loading. Here are the curious ones, the venturesome souls, and there is a land which is always visible across the water on clear days. The old people tell a story that very long ago many people had gone that way, that perhaps they went on still farther, beyond the land the Inuit could see from here. Now for a long time no one has gone, and the people have grown curious again.

Everything has been stowed in the bottom of the boat. Two solemn young men hold the bow steady in the lifting surf so that the tall one can look it all over and make sure all the necessary things are there. For quite a long time he stands there, taller than the others yet broad of shoulder, his keen eyes finding every last bundle. His square face is always calm and still, but today his thick lips are drawn tight. Here he is, leading people on a journey toward unknown places. He has to be absolutely sure they have the things they will need. Even his round-faced wife of the smiling lips is for once quiet and sober, standing there on the beach with a sealskin-wrapped bundle of clay dishes and lamps in her arms, the two children clinging to her. These people of his who, any other day, would have so much to say to one another are all standing there behind him, silent.

He nods at last, turns to his friends on the beach. Quickly they lift the three women, the two children, into the boat. Riding her husband's shoulder, the round-faced one reaches to take a last gift from the sister she is leaving behind, a bundle of fine small sinew for sewing. The sister stands knee-deep in the surf and holds it out to her, with tears rolling down over her plump cheeks.

Now there is a quick word from the leader. Out through the surf the boat shoots, the young men all leaping aboard. They are out beyond the surf in a moment, out on the slow blue waves, already separated from their people on the shore. The nine travelers each raise an arm in farewell. There is nothing to be said. Already they are too far away to be heard; the quiet watchers on the shore grow smaller, smaller.

Soon there is no fog at all and the quiet leader feels the spirits are going to be kind. Paddling steadily, the journeying ones can keep their eyes ever on their goal, the big island, whose bold jutting capes and headlands loom darkly blue in the distance. As in a dream the light skin-boat is rising and falling slowly with the waves, while all the daylight hours slide by.

The tall one holds the steering paddle strongly and smiles to himself; now that they are really on their way, he has a good feeling inside him. He looks over his boatload, most of them curled this way and that among the bundles, the two children in the bottom, little lumps under some skins, sound asleep. The women's heads are nodding on their breasts; that same motion, up and down, up and down, hour after hour, makes anyone drowsy, even adventurers on a journey to a new country. But one paddle never stops. It is the leader's. His young paddlemen can nod and paddle, and nod, wake and look at their two young wives, and nod again, but he is awake! He looks at his wife and smiles again; she is asleep too, at last, an arm still clasping her bundle of dishes, the most important things she owns. Poor woman, all worn out after the work of getting ready for such a journey as none of her people had ever thought of before. Ah well, they must be about halfway across now—no turning back!

He pulls from his belt a piece of dried mukluk seal and takes it in his lips. From the other side of his belt comes his sharp stone knife; with a swift upward motion the meat is cut off just under his nose. He chews and steers, and watches the flocks of gulls and murres wheeling and drifting back and forth over the water. A dark albatross on enormous motionless wings comes floating over the boat, and the man's eyes follow him.

The albatross sails over, turning a soft brown eye down on that queer thing bobbing about on the waves, no, not a whale this time, not a fish, something new in this world. He wheels away, and back again, to take another look, then skims off, low over the waves.

The half-dark hours of a spring night are rolling by. The light is coming back. The little boy squirms out from his warm nest and looks about with round mystified eyes. The man feels the dead sleepy weight pass from inside his head and looks ahead sharply. The big island now has highlands and peaks back from the shore, and shortly it has colors, red-brown high slopes, with paler outcroppings, inland, and great sweeps of tundra faint green, warm yellow and brown, spreading out from the mountains to the shore. Everyone is awake now, tossing back parka hoods, looking, looking. The paddles of the young hunters come alive again.

The leader points with his paddle to a great cape rising before them. Over and around its rock walls clouds of birds drift down like thick smoke. Food, clothing! The three women are chattering now!

Paddles are flying. On they speed close to the towering cliff, and on through the bay toward a fine hard beach. The surf is low and easy; but the boat's speed is checked beyond the first roller for a moment. Low murmur of voices. Is it a good landing in this strange place? Suddenly the tall one leans to his paddle with one long hard stroke. Up on the beach they go with a shout, "Oh—ho!"

Sevuokuk's first people have arrived!

He of the calm face knows of course what must first be done. The others stand, stiff, gazing wonderingly about, then wander curiously away up the shore, but he kneels on the beach well above the surf line. Beside him he has a tiny gutskin bag, and another made from the stomach of a seal. From the seal stomach he takes out his fire-making tools, a smooth board with a groove in it, a firestick with ivory mouthpiece, and a little bow. Now he opens the tiny bag and takes out a bit of crumbled sphagnum moss to lay beside the groove. Kneeling with back to the light wind, he closes his mouth over the ivory and begins twirling the stick with the bow. In a very little while he has a glowing bit of moss. This he empties gently into another little nest of moss and dry grass. Very gently he blows; the warm flames spring to life. Now he hears the others coming back. They are bringing driftwood.

Well enough! The first fire is ready to be fed.

Here had come the people who were to think the Island good, who were to remain and make it their own. Out of the Arctic mists had shone the Island, and into its mists at last have come the people to love it.

They have never heard of Rome or Britannia or Jerusalem. They themselves are The People, "Inuit." Their world is the Island, "Sevuokuk." Their lives are full.

This is their story.

. . . . .

Hunting and fishing and netting birds, gathering plants and seaweed, building houses of driftwood and whale ribs and sod, tramping the beaches, climbing over the hills, curing more hides, building more boats, more houses, making more tools—that is their story. And dancing through the long nights, telling old tales in snug houses on stormy days—that also is a part of the story.

Every summer more and more boats from the old home across the water were beached on Sevuokuk's shores and out of them came more people, live dogs, and many reindeer skins. After a time there were houses enough to be called a village, Sevuokukmeet, and Mioghokmeet, and more small villages all along the northern coast of the Island; wherever there was a beach and rocks where the seal and walrus could haul up, there was a camp, and across the island, forty miles away, grew a big village, Kukulik.

Yet the story is not all peaceful.

Some June morning in mist and rain came strangers in many skin-boats, and the peaceful dwellers on Sevuokuk discovered in blood and pain that these were not friends come to settle peacefully among them, not friends come peacefully to trade reindeer skins and willow and alder bark for walrus skins and rope and meat, but enemies, come to possess their good village sites, their hunting places. That meant war, war with bow and arrow and with spear, war by ambush and surprise. Women and children, huddled in the houses, were dragged out by victorious strangers and taken to new camps all along the coast.

The survivors were absorbed by the new people, people like them indeed, but from strange villages across the water. Mioghokmeet, Sevuokuk, Kukulik, all those villages were abandoned and silent, too empty of life, too full of skeletons, of ghosts, of unattached souls hovering over the place, shunned by victor and vanquished alike, frequented by the wild creatures of the island only, creatures who had known these places of old and had no concern for human doings.

The waves washed at the house doors, the snow sifted over them every winter. Yet summer after summer the blessed grass grew, until at last after hundreds of years, the sad villages would be gone, covered over by a smooth mantle of green.

Then, and then only, did the new mixture of people on Sevuokuk move back to the fine old hunting sites and build homes again on the very green mounds of their ancestors. So many generations had passed that the story had grown dim. They did not know that they were building on the bones of their forefathers. They knew only that this place, Sevuokuk, and that place, Kukulik, were the best places of all for quick and sure hunting, for protection from the harrying winds, for nearness to driftwood.

In the course of seventeen hundred years we know all this must have been repeated several times. More than once they must have been routed from their homes by warlike ones from more strange villages across the water. Once the strangers were on the shores it was impossible to defeat them, and after battle had died away, there would be the old home, abandoned still once more, and the new victors with their new slaves, afraid of the souls of those they had slain, and so going somewhere else to live. And all over again, the grass, the snow, the waves, taking over the village.

Even as they were conquerors this time, so would they be conquered at some other time, perhaps after so many years that everyone had forgotten about the last warfare. Life was full enough without fighting. So at last they made armor, and at last they knew they must swiftly attack any strange group who tried to land on their shores. Before the enemy could shove boats onto the beach they must be done away with, and they found that spears glanced impotently off of armor made of walrus hide hung with plates of ivory.

At last they were left alone, a mixed people, from many Siberian origins, but now one, the people of "Sevuokuk." And still there were among them descendants of those very first ones, so that the souls of those first brave ones still dwelt among the people.

The things the man had taught, the stories he had told in the winter evenings, the things his wife had been so careful to have done properly, the tools they had fashioned so skillfully, their fears, their customs, their laughter and their strength—these still dwelt among the people, through all the generations.

For the way their fathers had done, that was the way they must do always. A people living in fear of many unknowable things, a people wanting to laugh and find happiness, yet often beset by suffering—they must be sure to keep the spirits which govern all things pacified, in every action of their lives. So they must not leave the old way; things must be done thus and so and at proper times.

Island Between

THE SETTING

TIME   *About 1862.*

PLACE   *Sevuokuk Village, at the northwest corner of the Island.*

PEOPLE *In the House of Apangalook:*
Apangalook, hunter and leader
Assoonga, his wife
Toozak and Timkaroo, their sons
Tokoya and Sekwo, their daughters
Yokho, Assoonga's old mother
Ikmallowa, Apangalook's old father

In the House of Wohtillin:
Wohtillin, a leader also,
   Apangalook's older cousin
Rohltungu, his wife
Kotwowin, his old mother
Kulukhon, their older son
Tatoowi and Tongyan, sons

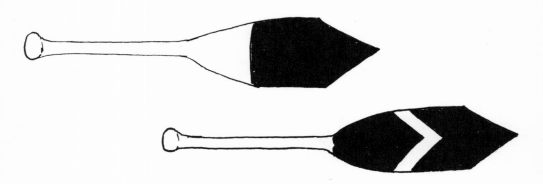

In the House of Pungwi:
Pungwi, the whale striker
Walla, his wife
Ega, their pretty daughter
Kaka and Okohoni, sons
Iyakatan, Pungwi's father,
  a wise old sorcerer

In the House of Yahoh:
Yahoh, the lazy one
Anatoonga, his young wife
Okoma, their daughter

Also these:
Ozook, another good whale striker
Walanga, his handsome son, a bad one
Irrigoo, another good hunter
Massiu, the young singer-sorcerer
Koonooku, a leader and rich man of
  Kukulik Village, across the Island
Mohok, Asha and Raganok, his wives
Kastevik, from Punuk Island

PART ONE
Being, Moon by Moon, a Year on Sevuokuk

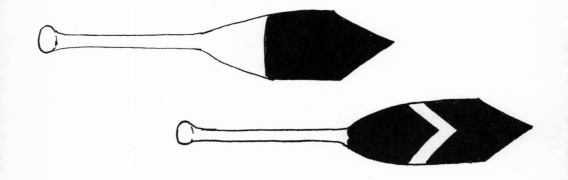

· KANAHYUNGASI ·
Moon of Frost Forming under the Roof

CHAPTER I

Coming of Siko

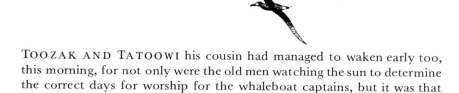

TOOZAK AND TATOOWI his cousin had managed to waken early too, this morning, for not only were the old men watching the sun to determine the correct days for worship for the whaleboat captains, but it was that exciting, uncertain time of year when the ice should be coming.

So up the Cape Mountain in the darkness before dawn, the two boys climbed, behind Wohtillin and Ikmallowa, toiling up its steep slope over icy rocks. Every morning at this time of year the two older men climbed the mountain. They had an important work up there.

In the dim light the great boulders on the mountain's top looked like dark giant people frozen fearsomely in place. The old men always dropped their voices when they spoke here, yet here was their place of vigil. They turned now, and, breathing heavily, stood watching the peaks and slopes of Powukpuk, inland to the east.

The ice was late, and the people were hungry. They were beginning to wonder whether somehow the spirits had been offended. Many times a day they had been climbing up the mountain to look and look. Now in the first light of morning the two older men and the two young ones stood still in a world where even the snow looked gray.

The dawn breeze which seems to whisper the secrets of departed spirits whipped the furs about the faces of the watchers. Toozak, so young, so curious, shifted restlessly and looked at Wohtillin. He had the same queer feeling inside that he always felt at a Worship—a kind of fear—a hope that they were doing the right thing, but always the fear that the spirits might not be satisfied.

Wohtillin and Ikmallowa stood calmly, yet on them lay the responsibility of numbering the days, for making sure the worships to the spirits of the animals, especially the maker of the whales, were held at the right time of the moon. And they did this by simply watching which peak of Powukpuk the sun touched first each morning! Toozak had of course been brought up to respect greatly the old people. Now he began to see why.

"When the sun is up a little more we should be able to see the ice if it is anywhere near us," murmured Ikmallowa. "Ay-yah, the light! On the third slope!"

Yes, there shone a glowing line along the northern slope of the third peak. "In four or five days more the moon will be right for holding whale worship in Pungwi's family, and in a few more days we will have Igo, the two stars, to help us tell time."

Wohtillin turned to Toozak, "You with the young eyes, can you see anything now in the north? It is almost light enough."

Toozak and Tatoowi both looked with all their power. Toozak crouched and cupped his hands about his cheeks and searched the northern horizon. Water, green and blue-black, rolling quietly to the sky which was becoming brighter each moment. Finally from Toozak came a deep, "Ah—ah-eh, look, Tatoowi, right there, see you anything?"

"Yes, yes, I see it now. Is it not so, Ikmallowa? Is it not the blink?"

The blink of Siko, the ice-pack! Not quite a halo in the sky just above the water, but a band, a faint shimmering veil of whiter than whiteness, low in the northern sky!

Those four watchers sprang into life! What greater thing than to be the bearers of good news? Toozak leapt like a fox from rock to rock, a warm flush rising clear to his scalp. He and Tatoowi were down over the rocky slopes first, but the old men were not far behind, to give real authority to the news.

"Siko—siko!" they shouted from the slope above the village, waving their arms. The people came pouring out of the houses, running to the shore to look, running up the slope to look, climbing up on the meat racks and meat cellar mounds to look. Tumult! Children racing up and down the slopes like wild squirrels, women standing in groups chattering and looking to the north. The four messengers were instantly the center of a group of leaders of the village. The information was officially received and discussed. Toozak tried not to show any feeling, but he did not miss the look his older brother Timkaroo gave him; there was a bit of respect in it.

Every eye was turned to the north. Siko, the great conveyor of life, was come again. Fears for empty stomachs, for the horrors of starvation, melt-

ed away in each heart; they were instantly happy, all. Laughter and exult-
ant voices rang along the shores. Food and clothing, fuel and bedding, tent
roofs, floor coverings, ivory for every kind of tool, ropes for lashing, all
floating toward them out of the rich north. Not merely life, but life with
joy and comfort, was assured to them for another year.

Toozak realized all this. But really the tremendous thing about it all was
that he, Toozak, had finally passed his sixteenth season of no-snow, and
now would be going upon the ice with the real hunters!

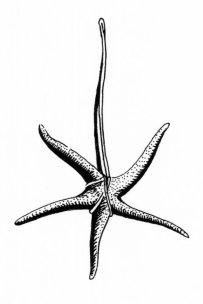

· KAHLOOVIK ·
Moon of Getting Tom-Cod with the Throwing Net

CHAPTER II

Siko and Iviek

TOOZAK opened his eyes just a little. Apangalook knelt there, shaking him, "Come boy, you cannot get Iviek in your sleep. The north wind still blows; everyone will be out on the ice. Assoonga has broth ready for us."

Toozak opened his eyes wide and scrambled out of his furs. In place of the dream fox running over the tundra, a great black walrus loomed in his mind. This was the day—perhaps this day he would become a hunter. Assoonga was there, smiling, holding out to her son trousers and sox of reindeer skin. He pulled them on. She brought outer trousers and boots of sealskin, tucking fresh insoles of dry grass into the boots, then came inner and outer parkas of deerskin and mitts of dogskin. Toozak pulled them all on in a dreamy manner, and with his thoughts running ahead of him out onto the ice, drank broth in the same manner.

All the hunters were setting out; from every house they came, tramping across the smooth shore ice of the cove, climbing like furry animals over the heaped rough ice the pack was fast piling up at the edge of the solid ice, and which was making a straight line between the two headlands of the village cove. Toozak hurried after his father and Timkaroo, Timkaroo, the already-experienced hunter. He had often enough mentioned that to Toozak. Toozak set his lips and hurried.

On the heaped ice ridge they stopped and gazed out at ice, solid fields of it, broken only here and there by small black pools of water between the angles of great floes. Otherwise there was simply whiteness, rough and glinting. The great pack had arrived. As far as they could see, the ocean had become a great white field, quiet and solid.

Apangalook jumped down onto the pack ice. He glanced back at the island; fog hung over the slopes, almost down to the beach, but out over the ice were gray clouds scudding along with the north wind. Toozak knew that his father would watch that fog; so long as it hung low, the wind was pushing the pack tighter and tighter against the island and hunters were safe on the ice.

Over the white field the men spread out, quietly, quickly, eyes busy. Each hunter carried on his back a sealskin bag. Through the cover of the bag lay a stout stick. In one hand he carried his harpoon, six feet of strong wood bound well with baleen, an ivory harpoon head already stuck into the plug in the end of it and fastened to the hundred-foot coil of walrus-hide rope which the hunter carried in his other hand. This coil was tied about in several places with short pieces of baleen, to keep it from springing wide open into a trap for the hunter.

Rapidly and silently they traveled. Toozak was breathing hard. He *would not* be the last one! Still, "No danger of that," he thought. He glanced quickly back over the ice and laughed aloud. "Yahoh the lazy one is far behind; here he comes, shuffling like a great bear, always the last one out on the ice, and the first one in at night! What would the people think if Yahoh came out first, one day?"

Toozak crawled cautiously over a jumble of broken ice and looked into an opening—black water with a clear green rim around its edge where it reflected the ice. Toozak noted all this but his attention was on a ripple in the water not far from him, a ripple which suddenly burst to release a huge bewhiskered face! Ongtopuk, the big male walrus!

He knew that Ongtopuk would only breathe once and go down again when he sensed something crouching there on the ice. Toozak's heart was pounding, but there were no other hunters very near and he got ready, poised, harpoon in hand, coil of rope thrown down on the ice. When Ongtopuk parted the black pool a second time, Toozak with one mighty thrust buried the harpoon head in that black muzzle.

Down went Ongtopuk with the five-inch piece of ivory deep in the soft flesh of his nostrils, and the hundred feet of rope began paying out swiftly, with the little baleen strips snapping as the rope broke them.

Yet swifter was Toozak. The instant he made his strike, the harpoon shaft was thrown behind him out of his way. He let out a great shout, "Come! Here is Iviek! Come quickly," even while he ducked his head and brought his sealskin hunting bag over it, onto the ice at his feet, pulled out the ivory-pointed stick from under its flap, and stuck the sharp point into the ice through the loop which marked the end of the curling rope. He knelt, holding that stick in the ice with all his strength.

All in an instant. In another instant Ongtopuk in his great rush had reached the end of the line, a great wounded hulk on the end of the line, with slender Toozak bearing back, his teeth set, then Timkaroo and Apangalook and many others there in a rush. Toozak's shout had brought them. Timkaroo knelt beside his brother, holding the stick. Apangalook stood ready with his own coil and harpoon. Quietly they watched. In a few seconds the poor whiskered face appeared again and received Apangalook's harpoon beside Toozak's, and they had another line on him. The next time, Timkaroo's harpoon drove home.

Ongtopuk was now desperate. With all this coming up and going down so quickly he had not been able to breathe properly. So at last he came up, blowing and snorting and breathing in great gasps; he simply must have more air. He could not go down again, and he hung there at the edge of the ice, a helpless creature. Apangalook handed his stone-tipped spear to Toozak. "Here, boy, it is your walrus. Strike for his heart."

Toozak took the spear, braced himself, set his teeth (Oh, to make a clean stroke with Timkaroo watching!), drove the point through that black side. Ongtopuk's mouth opened with a terrible roar and blood gushed in a great stream from his side. Toozak looked around at Timkaroo, a bit dazed. Timkaroo's eyes were full of thoughts. "You may be a hunter, some day," he murmured, and smiled.

Now the work had only begun. By this time there were more helpers. Stout Pungwi, clever with the ivory ice pick in one end of his harpoon shaft, began chopping a rope-hold in the ice twenty feet back from the edge; he soon had a hold under which the rope was led. Two others dug solid stances for their harpoons, one back from the ice-hold a few feet, one a little to the side and halfway to the edge. Apangalook, with Toozak watching carefully, had cut two big slits in the skin of Ongtopuk's head. Through this he tied one end of the rope and it was led around the two harpoons and under the hold in the ice, and now everyone began to pull, slowly, steadily, minute after minute, sweat pouring off their faces, until at last Ongtopuk, that great hulk, came slowly, slowly over the edge of the ice.

Apangalook made the first cut. With his stone knife he cut straight down the walrus's breast. There was nothing, thought Toozak, that his quiet father did not know how to do. They pulled out the stomach, a great bag, all that two men could manage. "But we fix that a little bit," laughed Pungwi. "Hunting has some pleasures."

Pungwi slit the stomach, reached in with bare hand and, grinning, pulled out juicy clams and mussels, all nicely shelled and steaming. Every hunter did the same, and squatting there on the ice, rested and feasted. "Ongtopuk ate well," laughed Apangalook. "Now we are hungry too. This stomach will soon not be too heavy for you to drag alone, Toozak, but drag it carefully; it will make a fine drum someday."

Apangalook licked the delicious juice from his fingers, pulled on his mitts. This was not the time to sit and tell stories. He set to work again, Toozak close beside him, watching and doing just as he did, pushing back for future pleasure the crowding thoughts of the big thing which had happened to him this day on the ice. Tonight, on the sleeping platform, he could live it all over.

The hide, the layer of fine blubber, a little meat underneath, these were the slabs they cut off, each one all that a man could drag on a rope. On each man's bag hung many little coils of mukluk rope for just this work. Trip after trip they made to the solid shore ice, depositing the meat; it would be divided among all who had helped haul Ongtopuk up.

Toozak's walrus was not the only one caught that day. The opening he had discovered was quite large and into it came walrus and seal from all about. Live in the water they could and did—swimming about in that dark world under the ice, but always watching their breathing holes; from far off they could see the light filtering down in certain places. This meant air and life to them and there they must go, often to find, with the air, not life, but death. Inuit were on the ice today, and they must have much meat, much oil, many skins, else the year could be horrible.

Of course Yahoh harpooned nothing, but he was on hand to hold a rope in his hands and appear to haul up several walrus. "I wonder," said Timkaroo to Toozak, "how he makes so much sweat pour down his face, when one cannot see his muscles move when we pull!"

"Oh, he uses a lot of strength grunting," answered Toozak quickly. "Didn't you hear? He grunted louder than anyone when Apangalook gave the signal to pull."

Toozak had a warm feeling inside. This was wonderful, Timkaroo laughing with him, Toozak, as with an equal! He even felt warm toward that fake, Yahoh. He had furnished the joke for them to laugh about together. Toozak bent fiercely to his work. "It is good to have a Yahoh, perhaps," he thought as he pulled a big slab along, "else we would have to search for something else for our fun."

People must always have fun.

The fog stayed over the mountains all day long. On the ice pack, with daring, with skill, with strength, with hard, hard work, the hunters kept steadily on. This was the time. Over the pack near every opening, walrus and big seals were hauled out just as Toozak's had been hauled.

Timkaroo left the meat cutting long enough to harpoon a fine ribbon seal[1] at a small breathing hole, and that was a great thing, for the pretty things would be there in the pack only a few days and then they would not be seen again until they came in spring, traveling north. Toozak saw his brother hauling the beautiful seal rapidly to shore.

Ah-hah! Timkaroo is not feeling the sting of this bitter north wind right now. He is thinking only of what a fine present he has for that round-faced Ega. Such a clothes-bag should make her feel warm toward him.

While the north wind held, there was no rest. Toozak finally added the walrus stomach to the growing pile of meat on the solid shore ice. He noticed that up on the shore old Ikmallowa and Iyakatan were slowly walking, up and down, standing a bit, walking again, always watching. They were the guardians; they had a task, watching the ice, the sky, the currents, the wind. So long as hunters were out there some older men would be watching from shore.

Toozak trudged back to the walrus again. Timkaroo was pulling out the great length of intestine, running his hand along it, squeezing the contents out upon the ice. He then took the hundred-foot-long tube, divided it in three, braided it; now it was ready to be carried home and hung up until Assoonga needed it for rain parkas and snowshirts.

Timkaroo looked up into the weary young face and laughed, "Ho, hunter boy, lots of fun to get Ongtopuk, eh? And lots of work too! Warm ningloo will feel pretty good tonight. Here is your walrus heart. What is happening?"

From beyond them they heard a shout, taken up from group to group and followed by sudden motion in every place. Timkaroo grasped his brother's arm and pointed. Over on the shore the two old men were slowly waving their white snowshirts and the hunters also could see now the fog was breaking and lifting.

"We have plenty of time yet," said Timkaroo. "They are waving *slowly*. But come along."

From far out over the pack, gray-white now in the deepening dusk, bulky black figures came, dragging slabs of precious meat behind them. The two old men stood still and waited; bitter cold it was for them, but they would watch until every hunter was safe on the shore ice. A good day on the ice would then be finished and along with the weary hungry hunters they too would go to the warm ningloos. The women would be waiting to help them out of sweat-soaked, ice-hung clothing and to serve them good food.

Toozak almost staggered across the rough ice, but his heart was glowing. He had made his first big catch and now was qualified to go upon the ice, able to care for himself, and his brother was treating him as an equal. He came up to the old men, and his grandfather, Ikmallowa laid a hand on his shoulder. "Ah, so here is a new hunter, carrying home his first head of Iviek!"

Ikmallowa, by his words, had accepted Toozak the boy as Toozak the man. Nothing more could be added to this day!

Yet when the men were rid of their wet clothes, Toozak and his father, weary as they were, must still do one more thing. They carried in the great tusked head of Ongtopuk from the passageway and laid it by the center-post. Behind them came Assoonga, carrying a little wooden bowl in which was some nunivak, the green tundra plant, and Tokoya, kneeling, took a pinch of greens from the bowl and placed it between the walrus's lips while all the others stood silent. Thus was the walrus spirit fed and appeased and more walrus in future hunting assured to Toozak.

So also must the house idol be fed. As after every ceremony, Tokoya now rose and crossed over to the front wall of the house where hung the carved wooden man with his hungry, smiling teeth. She rubbed a bit of nunivak against these clenched teeth, her long braids hanging back from her smooth round cheeks as she reached up. Toozak, tired as he was, noticed that his sister was becoming good to look at.

At last they could rest and eat and become warm clear through. What delicacies Ongtopuk provided! Clams from his paunch, slices of mangona, heart and liver and kidneys. The young folks could not eat any of the heart, lest they get bad sores from little scratches, but in the big platter, and in plenty, were other fine things. From the cheeks of the walrus Assoonga cut rich slices, being careful not to cut near the lips of course, for that would cause the lips of him who ate that part to twitch, and likewise she was careful not to get too near the ear, for the spirit who sent the meat to their shores must not be rendered deaf to their prayers.

"Did you bring in the breast bones? Ah, those soft bones, they are fine to chew!"

"Yes, we brought in everything good," answered Apangalook. "See, here is the last rib; that is a good one. Toozak, be careful not to eat near this rib, else you will have pains in your side when exercising." Apangalook laughed as he took the piece of rib and bit off juicy bites of raw meat. He smacked his lips loudly. Such good food deserved proper appreciation. He had forgotten cold and the weariness of long hours on the ice.

He looked about at his family, squatted in a happy circle on the floor about the platter. Heat and glow from two lamps in the corners made everything comfortable. There was Ikmallowa, worn, almost nodding over his meat, but content after his long watch; there was Assoonga's lively little old mother Yokho, cutting up a piece of liver and feeding choice bits to fat little Sekwo, who accepted all the nice bites her grandmother handed her in an absent-minded manner, all the while gazing in round-eyed wonder at her brother Toozak, who had suddenly become a hunter and left his boyhood behind. Apangalook watched Sekwo's eyes and smiled. He too could gaze with proud eyes at his sons, so quickly had they changed from small boys swinging bird bolas and netting crabs to strong men able to hold their own on the ice. Any father would feel good!

Apangalook's eyes went clear round the circle, back to his Assoonga of the happy glance, busy cutting more pieces of heart on the end of the platter, and Tokoya, round and supple and smooth of skin. His family, well fed, in warmth and safety. Apangalook was well satisfied this night.

CHAPTER III

Ahrolah, the Dance

"TOKOYA," Toozak thrust head and shoulders through the entrance-way, "There is going to be dancing tonight; the people will all come here because this is the largest house. Tell Assoonga; I go to the other houses."

The quick words faded away as Toozak backed out through the entrance. Tokoya jumped from the floor and bundled up the murre-skin parka she was making and stowed it away in her own sleeping place. Assoonga was bustling about right away. She was pushing back the neatly rolled up skins on the sleeping platform and moving the two lamps back.

Tokoya began sweeping the floor with a goose wing. Little Sekwo hopped about before her, gathering up scraps of mouse skins; she had been making a parka for her ivory doll. Old Yokho of the bright smile leaned over from her high sleeping platform over the entrance. "Get every scrap picked up, small girl, and let Tokoya put all into the bag. The spirit who might wish you harm cannot then find anything of you outside to cast a spell upon. You, Tokoya, are becoming a swift worker; I wonder if that smiling white-toothed son of Wohtillin's will be stealing looks at someone tonight."

Yokho laughed; Tokoya and Sekwo giggled. Tokoya swept the scraps carefully into the gutskin bag and pushed it far back under the sleeping platform at the back of the room. Surely no wandering evil spirit could see it there.

Assoonga looked about with a careful eye. "Here, Tokoya, help me move these pots and platters back under here; people cannot dance in meat platters."

At this thought they all laughed; anticipation and festivity had already taken possession of the house of Apangalook.

Now the house was clear; they must make themselves ready. Tokoya took her little towel of finely stripped grass from the swinging rack, pulled the urine tub out from under the platform, knelt and sponged herself carefully. Then from under her bed of skins she drew forth a fine soft piece of sealskin, and, having changed her old kalevak for this, she pulled its drawstring of seal thong about her, just below her waist, and tied it tightly.

Sitting on a little stool of whale vertebra, she combed and combed her shiny long hair with her ivory comb and plaited it in two smooth braids, inserting in each one a hair button of choicest orange ivory, finely carved in radiating lines. These were her best buttons; Apangalook had finished them only a few nights before, and Tokoya was glad she had such a good occasion to wear them for the first time. Now she was ready.

Yokho, lying on her own special platform above the entrance, where it was always warm, watched all this below, with Sekwo curled up beside her. She remembered well all the nights in years gone by when she, Yokho, had been always the first chosen to dance, the first to be loved. She had had her full share of all that; she knew what life brought. Tonight she could be up here where the warmth eased the ache in her old bones, and could watch and smile at youth. "Tokoya," she called softly. Tokoya lifted her big serious eyes to her grandmother. "Tokoya, will you smile at Wohtillin's son tonight when no one is looking? I am sure he is the one your father will betroth you to. You are surely not going to be like the sea lion?"

"Sea lion!" gasped Tokoya, and Sekwo, playing with some old hair buttons, squealed, "Sea lion, oh ho, Grandmother says you are like sea lion!"

"Yes, the sea lion was once a girl like you, you know," answered Yokho.

Once there lived a man who had a daughter who refused to marry any of the youth of the neighborhood. Every young man worked for her but she did not pay any attention to any of them. Her father scolded her for refusing. He tied a piece of strong rawhide around her ankle and fastened the other end to a cliff nearby. She was hanged down.

Sometime afterward, the people launched their boats to hunt for birds for clothing and meat. When the first boat came by, the girl cried out, "Oh, young man, come and let me loose and I shall marry you."

But the young man told her that he would never marry her. One by one the boats passed by and she cried the same way to each of them, but each of them made the same answer.

At last the girl's own parents came along. When she saw them she kicked with all her might and broke the hide and fell right into the water. When she came up she was formed into a sea lion. She came up near her father and pulled the skin off her face. The father saw that it was his daughter and told her to come up into the boat. She told him she would not for she had been treated roughly by him. She then replaced the skin on her face, and upsetting the boat, swam after the boats, chasing them. When she came to a boat she came up on one side and upset the boat. She did this for their refusing to help her. After that she never changed her form any more.

Now the people believe the sea lion was once a girl and for that reason the sea lion often stays at the cliffs most of the time.

Tokoya stood up and lifted her mouth close to her grandmother's ear. "I am not going to be a sea lion," she whispered.

Then Assoonga called, "Here are people."

Low voices, laughing, whispering. In came Apangalook, followed by all the older people of the village.

Tokoya slipped into her birdskin parka and joined the other young people out in the entrance-way. Here in the dark they crowded together in a warm close group, looking upon the scene within, where the room was lit by three lamps into yellow light and deep shadow.

Sleeping platforms on either side were packed with mothers and babies and older people; on the platform across the back of the room the five drummers sat cross-legged; the yellow glow shone on them, on shining intent faces bent above the white drums of walrus stomach stretched over round frames, on bare gleaming shoulders and thighs.

Suddenly they all lifted their drums as one and the song started, "Ah-hh, yunga ya, hunga ha, ha-ha."

Tokoya always wondered how a singer kept from hitting himself in the face. He held the stick in his left hand, the flat drum in the right, and beat the drum upon the stick, swinging it close to his face on each upswing. She watched the singers intently, but she knew all the time that Wohtillin's son Kulukhon was standing very close behind her.

She saw Ikmallowa reach over and touch Wohtillin, amid cries of approval from all around the room. Wohtillin, that stout, square-shouldered one, slipped out of his parka and stepped to the center of the room, facing the singers. On went the song, Wohtillin crying out at the singers now and then as though answering them, moving his arms and feet slowly, carelessly.

Suddenly a loud cry from all, the drums were held high above the singers' heads, and the song and the beat crashed into a fast, frenzied speed. Everyone in the room leaned forward, tense; the older men cried out in high voices, and Wohtillin was transformed into a wild spirit, hands, feet, body, face and voice, all were changed. Crouching and springing, rippling the muscles of his shining bare shoulders and grimacing fiercely, he was now a wild venomous spirit, now a terrified soul praying mercy. And, as suddenly, it ended, in the very midst of a fierce gesture, arms above head. Wohtillin might be getting old, but still he was one of the best dancers, just as he was still a good whale striker.

Only a short pause, and the singers began again; now it was Pungwi's turn. Here, there, with quick stiff motions Pungwi danced, with stiff knees and stiff elbows, but so fast, when the music changed, that he was all one motion, faster and faster came the drumbeats, faster and faster went the dancer. The whole roomful was singing and swaying now, all the parkas were off, warmer and warmer grew the air. Shoulders and breasts gleamed with sweat and oil.

"Toom-toom, toom-toom," all traveled together on the urgent rhythm of the drums, and then again, on a sudden high cry from Pungwi, all ceased. Pungwi went to his seat breathing hard.

So it went on and on, until Apangalook pointed to the doorway full of young faces. Here were fine dancers. Each had his own dance, but they must not venture in until called for by the older people. A babble of voices answered Apangalook's gesture. "Yes, call in the young hunter who does the walrus dance. Call in the shy girl who does the nunivak dance."

So two and three at a time they were called in. Some dances were very solemn; some were wildly funny. Timkaroo was a walrus crawling up onto a shelf of ice. Everyone rocked and howled with laughter at him. Toozak was a murre getting ready to dive off his ledge of rock into the breakers, and never had he danced with such wild force. For he was a hunter now. Life had all become different in the last few days. Everything he did was done with all his force.

But Massiu was a tormented soul brushing away evil spirits. All of these things were a part of life and must be expressed in dance.

Apangalook had brought in an extra block of ice, so that over two of the lamps hung ice, dripping into clay pots for drinking water. In every lull the water was passed around. The singers needed more energy then any of them; they drank and drank, and each time spat on their drums and rubbed them all over so they would not dry out.

"The nunivak dance," someone cried, and now at last Tokoya must come in, slip off her parka and stand there in the soft light before the singers, her braids hanging almost to her knees.

Slowly they began, as always; Tokoya's feet never moved, but knees and arms swayed gracefully with the music. Then the crash of drums and the loud cry, and suddenly, how supple and swift was Tokoya, sweet shy face lowered always, but from her ankles up all one live feeling, bending and swaying, picking greens from the tundra, arms and shoulders moving in perfect abandon with the wild call of the song. As suddenly as did the others her dance ended, she stood with arms flung out, the nunivak all gathered. For one instant she raised her eyes and there was Kulukhon gazing right at her, oblivious of etiquette, a strange rapt expression in his eyes. Tokoya hurried out to the doorway, eyes down, but something had traveled from Kulukhon to her and back again.

And there was that Toozak, whose eyes saw all things. When he was younger the other children had teased him about this. "Toozak, he sees everything," they would cry. "He sees the lemmings in their holes and the seals under the ice."

But it was not such a bad thing, to see what went on! He saw Kulukhon stealing glances at his sister all night long; he saw the look pass between them at the end of her dance. That was amusing. What was *not* amusing was that Walanga, that handsome one of the narrow eyes, was also gazing at Tokoya all evening, and he had no right. Toozak was puzzled. He looked back at Kulukhon, standing there with his usual sweet, good-natured smile, more good-natured than ever, in fact. "He sees nothing but Tokoya; someone else, with eyes not asleep, will have to see his troubles *for* him," decided Toozak.

But it turned out that Kulukhon had two helpers. Tatoowi, the lively one, poked Toozak and hissed in his ear. "Have you had eyes in your head tonight? You may possibly have seen some narrow ones looking where they should not."

"Are my eyes usually asleep?"

The two curious young ones glanced quickly about the roon, then blankly at the dance. Tatoowi kept on whispering. "I have heard Ikmallowa say that to share one's wife with a friend or guest at times was only a part of hospitality, but that a third person between a pair only *betrothed*—that meant trouble."

CHAPTER IV

For a Wife

APANGALOOK looked at his old friend Wohtillin's face when he came through the entrance-way and knew there was a matter of importance to be talked over. Together they crossed to the far corner by the lamp where Assoonga sat sewing, and the talk began in low tones.

As for Tokoya, she pulled on her boots and parka and hurried out. She walked through the village slowly. An icy fog hung over everything but Tokoya was deep in her fur hood and deep in her thoughts too. She knew what was going on back there. She was being formally betrothed to Kulukhon. It had been an understood thing for years, but now that the time had come she wondered. She wondered whether she could ever love a husband as she did her own family. Of course, every woman had to have a husband, and Kulukhon was strong and clever, son of a good hunter and proved as one himself.

She found herself at the far end of the village, staring into a thick white wall of fog. No hunters out today; no children rolling in the snow with puppies; no dogteams coming in from traplines. She was alone here in a white world, and strange it was, with no wind stirring, only silence and the fog. Gazing into that fog, she suddenly remembered Kulukhon's face, his eyes as they had looked straight into hers the night of the dance, and she felt again that strange feeling, that pleasant fear. It was puzzling.

Now from this day on she knew they must ignore each other wherever they were, never looking at each other, never acknowledging the other's presence, at least, not when anyone might see!

Not many days passed before they were all roused from their work near the end of the day by sounds beyond the passageway, voices, then one voice. Toozak balanced a half-finished harpoon point on his hand and watched the entrance-way. Ah, he *thought* he had known that voice. It was that brisk and talkative Walla, Pungwi's wife, cousin to Apangalook. "And on no common visit is she come this time, I think," said Toozak to Tokoya. "You might be able to guess."

He made a sly face and aimed the harpoon point at his sister. Tokoya said nothing, slid way back on her sleeping platform and started combing her hair as though she had no interest in what went on. But Toozak listened!

Solemnly, dressed in her best parka, Walla stood before Apangalook. "I speak for your friend Wohtillin who waits outside. He and his family bring betrothal gifts to you. They wish to seal the betrothal of one who is your daughter to Wohtillin's son, Kulukhon. Will you come out?"

Apangalook glanced at Assoonga, calmly sewing beside the lamp. He and Walla stooped into the passageway. Toozak quietly followed. It was just as well to see all one could in this life. Outside, he stayed quietly in the background, so as not to disturb the ceremony.

The men who had hauled the long sled stood silently by while Apangalook and Wohtillin handled each article in the load and Apangalook took plenty of time to examine everything carefully. Now and then Walla said a word in admiration of some gift. It wasn't very often a woman had the privilege of speaking with men. She might as well make the most of it.

This was what Wohtillin thought Tokoya was worth, and a goodly payment it was, of things Apangalook could well use—two rolls of new dried walrus skins for ungiak covers, three rolls each of new walrus and mukluk rope, carefully coiled and tied, two new reindeer skins from across the water, ivory arrowheads, a bird dart and a seal dart, and a supply of ivory harpoon heads, which Wohtillin could make better than anyone else, and which Apangalook had long admired.

Of course it was understood that after Kulukhon and Tokoya were really married, perhaps after they had had a child, he would take her home to his father's house to live, and Apangalook would send with her gifts equal to those Wohtillin now brought for the betrothal.

"So," thought Toozak, "now we shall have Kulukhon in my father's boat crew, and bringing all his catch to this house. Now he starts really to work to pay for a wife."

He saw his father nod and smile at Wohtillin, and motion the men to carry in the gifts. He could come forward now and help carry things. He lifted two coils of rope off the sled and glanced across at the house of Ozook. Some movement there had caught his eye. And so quick was that eye that

Toozak was positive he saw fierce unguarded hatred in the face of Walanga, peering out of his father's passageway at this ceremony going on. Now he was gone, but Toozak carried his load into the house with a frown on his face. Ikmallowa, wise old man, had said, "It can happen in any village that there is one who does not wish to follow the law."

Early one morning there was a shout from the outer end of the passageway, "Is there a woman within who will receive Noghsuk?"

Assoonga poured a little water into a small baleen bucket and hurried out through the passageway. Kulukhon stood there, frost and ice hanging from his clothes, a large spotted seal at his feet. "I have brought a seal to my future father-in-law," he announced.

He stooped and turned the seal so that the head pointed in to the entrance. Assoonga lifted the bucket and dashed water over its mouth and head. Thus the soul of the seal would see that the seals were treated kindly by giving them of their native element, and the great maker of the seals would feel kindly toward Inuit hunters.

Assoonga smiled at the young hunter, and he followed her into the house, carrying his catch. Tokoya sat on the floor, bent over her sewing. Her hair was newly braided with many ivory charms, but of course she did not lift her eyes.

Toozak was supposed to be mending a sealskin dog harness, but he could still see all that went on about him, and the actions of those two were amusing to watch. This night, perhaps, Kulukhon would come into this house bearing his sleeping robes and Apangalook would give him a place on the sleeping platform next to Toozak. Tokoya slept across the room, beside little Sekwo. These were the first steps toward marriage.

Toozak wondered how Timkaroo was getting along. He had been gone for several weeks now, sleeping in the house of Pungwi, father of that desirable round-faced Ega.

. . . . .

Day after day on the ice. Toozak almost wished he hadn't so quickly grown to be a hunter, and was really glad when a south wind came and they had to stay off the ice for a few days, though no one could have made him speak such a thought.

It was almost dark this day as he came home from a crab netting trip to the cape with Tatoowi. Almost dark, yet he did not think his eyes had failed him. He stopped near the meat rack and there was Tokoya, pulling down strips of dried mukluk. "Darkness is kind to those who fear light," he murmured in her ear.

Tokoya turned quickly, her eyes snapping. "If you mean you saw something with those busy eyes of yours, it was that soft-footed Walanga. He must have heard you coming, or he would still be here."

She paused, breathing quickly, touched Toozak on the sleeve. "I do not understand him, and I do not want him near me. He speaks in strange phrases, too. 'Hungry birds that flit about at night'—what sense does that make?" and Tokoya pulled down a last strip of meat and stalked away to the house.

Toozak let only half of himself sleep that night. At the first tiny strange sound, he was all awake. He turned his head slowly. Kulukhon was still there beside him, tired out by a long day on the ice trapline, sleeping soundly. So it was not he, looming there just inside the entrance.

Toozak's eyes were busy but he lay as one dead. The black figure passed between him and the tiny glow of the one wick left burning and Toozak knew the hungry profile of Walanga. Very slowly and silently it moved, half crouching, across toward Tokoya's sleeping place.

"Birds that flit about in darkness, eh?" thought Toozak, his lips twitching. "This could be very bad, but this time I think it will be only funny!"

The house of Apangalook was suddenly filled with a horrible roar, the roar of Ongtopuk the big male walrus. "Ah-ooh-oogh-oogh! Ooogh, the harpoon is in me—oogh, ow-oogh!"

What a noise!

"Toozak, wake up, wake up, what is the matter?" Kulukhon's arms were about him, shaking him. Assoonga and Tokoya were crying out in fright, Assoonga reached to trim the lamp and make a brighter light to see what all the trouble was, and Apangalook had sprung out into the middle of the room. Toozak looked all about and saw their wide startled eyes in the yellow glow. He gasped and blinked as though just waking.

"Oh, what was it? Ah-eee, I am sorry to have wakened everyone, but ay-yah, that was funny! I thought I was Ongtopuk and somebody had a harpoon in me. Ha,ha,ha, wheee—what a dream!"

And Toozak lay back, choking with laughter. Oh, funny world! Too bad Kulukhon hadn't wakened quickly enough to see how fast that Walanga had gotten out of there!

CHAPTER V

The Singer

TOOZAK AND TATOOWI and some of the others stood outside the entrance of Massiu's home. No one made a sound.

From the house came a strange chanting, not a song but a queer succession of sounds, of grunting like an animal, crying like one whose soul was leaving him, of moaning like the south wind in the cliff caves. It was not Massiu's voice, but the voice of one possessed by strange spirits, and for three days it had been going on this way.

The boys standing there looked afraid and bewildered, but old Ikmallowa spoke quietly. "Massiu is to become a sorcerer. In a few days this strange spirit will leave him and he will be as Massiu again but will have the power of singing. He will be a Singer as his father Iakitan was, as Nuganum of Kukulik village is. Wait and see. He will have the power to sing demons from our sick and to bring the seal and the walrus to our shores. It is well."

A few days later little Sekwo awoke in the night moaning and crying, with hot cheeks. Assoonga knelt beside her with tears streaming down her cheeks, and old Yokho spoke softly to Apangalook, "Some evil spirit has entered this house. Sekwo's soul has perhaps strayed away. You had best bring Massiu."

Massiu was taller than the other young men, and slender. He was Massiu again, as before his possession, but quieter, as one in authority. The family all retired to the platform at the back of the house when he came in; all but Apangalook, who must first arrange the payment for the Singer's services. And Toozak the curious one, of course lay wide awake in his own place, listening, watching. He heard Massiu's soft voice:

"You will perhaps be glad to bring me a new sealskin and one slab of walrus?"

41

Apangalook nodded. Toozak knew his father would gladly pay that and much more to have the pet of the family made well. He knew, too, that if ever they needed Massiu's services in the future, the payment must be the same, else the spirits would be upset.

Massiu pulled the covers from Sekwo's feverish face, smoothed her forehead with slow fingers, and began to sing in a very low, sweet tone:

"Close your eyes and listen, small girl. Go, devil, go; come, soul, come, come back to your rightful home."

Softly, swaying over the sick child's bed, then louder and louder, and low again, now whispering a secret formula, now crying aloud, flinging his arms out to push away the demon, holding out hands to call the absent soul back, so Massiu kept on. Sekwo slept fitfully, still moaning in her sleep. Her round cheeks were still too warm.

Toozak did not sleep. He lay there, wondering. There was Massiu, only a few weeks ago a gay, careless playmate of his, and now so different. At least he acted different. And all these chants Massiu's father had made him learn! Toozak remembered how Massiu had laughed and made fun of them when he had to learn them. Now since those three days of strange illness he was singing them with such a solemn face. Toozak wondered. It must be as Ikmallowa said; there were spirits everywhere, and only one possessed in some strange way could talk with them. Spirits in water, in air, in the winds, spirits in birds and in all animals; greatest of all was the spirit of the whale, that great spirit called Keyagunuk.

"I wonder what they look like," thought Toozak drowsily. Massiu's voice was putting him to sleep—

Suddenly, silence flowed into the dark house, upon all the listeners. Toozak started up too. Massiu had stopped, head thrown back, eyes staring wide. In a faraway voice Massiu sang, "The spirits bid you sacrifice a dog; the evil will enter the dog and go with him, leaving the child. Go and mark him now."

Apangalook rose and looked at the Singer, looked at old Yokho, leaning from her sleeping place. She nodded. He swiftly pulled on his clothes, and Toozak did likewise. When his father left the house, Toozak was at his heels. Outside, Apangalook walked over to gentle old Kikmik, mother of many of his finest dogs. Toozak had feared this very thing—a cold heavy lump was inside him as he followed his father. Apangalook turned and looked at his young hunter, "I know she is your old friend, but she is the only one I can spare."

They stood a moment looking down at Kikmik. Kikmik wagged her bushy tail and wiggled all over and jumped about Toozak's feet. Apangalook sighed; he was not a hard man. "You, Kikmik, must take the anger of the spirits upon you for our little daughter."

He took out his stone knife and slit Kikmik's ear and through it pulled a narrow strip of sealskin. He and Toozak straightened and looked toward the mountain; the point of the Dipper swung in the south and they knew it was soon morning. The air was cold with the ghostly cold of dawn; the wind was blowing loose snow about in icy gusts. They could barely recognize the face of Pungwi, who came suddenly through the snow. "You are marking a dog?"

Apangalook nodded. Pungwi turned back. Instead of going out to look for seals, Pungwi would now notify all the people. They would stay in their houses and not look about until the sacrifice was over. That was only courtesy.

Now, inside the house, Massiu and Assoonga had raised Sekwo from her bed and were holding her standing, between them. The sick one made never a sound but her head hung sadly against her mother's arm. First came Ikmallowa, and, first raising one foot and then the other, he wiped both carefully on Sekwo's clothing. From shoulder to boot he passed each foot, then stood back to let the next relative do the same thing. All evil spirits must be gotten into one place.

Assoonga and Ikmallowa now came through the entrance, half carrying Sekwo between them. Apangalook led Kikmik out in front of the group, laid her on her back, knelt over her and stabbed her with one clean stroke of his stone knife. Kikmik was gone. Apangalook cut off her ears and handed them to Massiu, who tossed them into the air with a murmured formula. The family all stood quietly while Apangalook slit the body open and pulled out the intestines. Toozak was shaking with cold and misery, but he stood there quietly. Ikmallowa came forward and the two older men held the intestines up as high as they could over the dead Kikmik.

Then Assoonga and Toozak led little Sekwo, moaning softly, head hanging low, through the intestine loop. Behind them came the rest of the family, stepping under the loop also, to gain protection from whatever demon of sickness had caused Sekwo's soul to stray away.

When all had passed under the loop, they walked silently back into the house. Apangalook would have lifted the body of Kikmik, but Toozak was there first. Carrying his old friend tenderly, he moved out into the winter mist and swirling snow of the tundra.

Sekwo lay shivering between the furs, but the red was gone from her cheeks and as Massiu's low chant went on again, she fell asleep quietly. "Now her soul has come back," whispered Massiu. His work was done.

Toozak came through the entrance again, beating the snow from his clothes. He brought Massiu his parka and helped him into it silently, a bewildered respect in his eyes.

Yes, it must be that Massiu had gone far beyond his boyhood doings. He would go home now, and Apangalook would soon come dragging the slab of walrus and the sealskin. Kikmik was gone, but Sekwo had gotten her soul back.

· NAHZEGHOHSEK ·
Moon of Approaching of
Young Seal

CHAPTER VI

Winter Festival

TOOZAK was loading the sled, and the dogs were jumping and yelping in harness. So were all the other dogs in the village. Every family was getting ready to start for Kukulik and the big winter festival. There was plenty of noise.

Sekwo, well and bright-eyed once more, climbed onto the sled and poked her fat fingers into all the rolls and bundles. "And Grandmother and cousin Notangi and I have to stay home all alone! See, I could squeeze right down here and no one would know I was along."

"Hi," cried Toozak, "why do you want to go to a winter festival? All your friends will still be here. Don't you know this is the grown people's festival? This is the first time Tatoowi and I have ever been allowed to go. Move off now so I can lash this load."

Over into a snowdrift rolled Sekwo, and sat there hugging a black and white puppy in her arms. "Tell me then about this Koonooku. Is he greater than our father Apangalook?"

"No, not bigger or wiser," answered Toozak, throwing a mukluk thong lashing across the load, "but Koonooku has lately been favored by the spirits, it seems. He has been growing rich. He was the most fortunate of all the whaling captains last spring, and in June, the walrus, they say, followed his ungiak. During July and August he and his people got many fish at the island fishing streams, and on the big lagoon they caught geese and ducks of all kinds. He is even rich enough to have three wives now."

Toozak glanced across to Pungwi's house, where Tatoowi was helping load his father's sled, and acting pretty important about it, too, Toozak thought. "And as though that were not enough for Koonooku," Toozak went on, "the month of freezing brought a great run of fish of the ocean, when the slush ice formed along the shores at Kukulik. Koonooku's meat cellars are bursting with all kinds of good food, and his meat racks loaded with bundles of skins of walrus, seals and birds. Yes, Koonooku has become the great man of that village."

Toozak tied the last knot, placed his beautiful new parka, rolled carefully inside out, under the top lashing, where it would not get rubbed. He was glad Koonooku had chosen this time to prove his greatness by bidding the whole island to a great festival of giving.

Now came Assoonga and Tokoya, in their best new winter clothes, and climbed on top the load. Apangalook came out last, also in the finest of new clothes, and gave the word to the eager dogs. Pungwi's team had just pulled out. Teams were starting off all through the village, dogs yelping and crying, spreading out across the frozen lake at the foot of the Cape Mountain like a great wing.

· · · · ·

Into Kukulik team after team came trotting in the snowy half-dark of a winter day. In every house two lamps burned high and the eager low voices, the soft laughter, went on without pause until the very walls seemed to hum. Each Kukulik family had a houseful of relatives and friends from other parts as guests. Many they had not seen for a year, many not since August, when the fall storms had commenced and the boats no longer visited along the north coast between the two villages.

Apangalook's family were entertained in Koonooku's own house. It was only fitting. Apangalook was the best hunter, the wisest man, from Sevuokuk village.

Toozak and Tatoowi found themselves on the boy's platform at the back of the big house, their Kukulik cousins sitting close about them. They all spoke in low voices, because there were older people talking in the house. Toozak and Tatoowi soon noticed that these hosts of theirs had no more stupendous happenings to tell about than they, the guests from Sevuokuk, could relate if they wished. Only one of the boys had been to hunt on the ice, and then got only seals. Toozak wasn't going to start chattering about himself in a strange house, but he let slip a phrase or two which led them to suspect strongly that he, Toozak, had got Ongtopuk on his very first day on the ice! His young hosts looked at him with many feelings spread upon their faces. "Oh, it is so," chimed in Tatoowi, "my brother helped to haul the great thing up."

The honor of Sevuokuk village must be upheld, here in Kukulik.

Toozak leaned back on his bundle of robes more comfortably now and felt quite at home. Below them, on the floor about the cooking lamps, his mother and Tokoya were talking busily with the wives of Koonooku's household, but quietly too, for the men must not be disturbed.

Koonooku's oldest wife, little Asha, stirred her pots of walrus broth and braided seal intestines and seal meat in an absent manner, her attention on the talk going on all about her. Toozak nudged Tatoowi. "Look at them. They are as excited over their gossip of sewing and babies and sickness and betrothals as our fathers are over their talk of storms and traps and hunting."

Tatoowi laughed, "Yes, they are learning a new stitch for a boot or a new way to cook seal and greens. Oh well, my new parka feels very comfortable, and the braided seal intestines and walrus smell good. Women do well enough."

The house was warm, and the men's talk and women's quick low murmur and the little snorts and giggles of the young boys all mingled in the warm wave of comfort and good smells from the clay pots. In this being together there was a warm feeling of happiness.

Added to the happiness there was also anticipation of pleasures to come. Not only were they all come together to visit and exchange news, not only were they each to receive a portion of Koonooku's wealth, but this was also the festival of exchange. When the good things had been eaten in each house, every woman began making herself ready for the dance at Koonooku's home, and each of them knew, as she sat in some corner combing her hair and braiding it with her finest charms and buttons, that she would not that night be with her own husband, but with some other woman's; that some other woman would be with *her* husband. Such was the custom. So had their parents and grandparents done at the big winter festivals.

The men came into the big house of Koonooku first, crawling through the passageway and sitting down quickly, for to stay on one's feet in a house means a challenge to the host, and by all means they meant to use their best manners at a festival like this. The young men sat around on the floor, and the old men, like a group of judges, sat on the rear platform above the musicians. Toozak and Tatoowi, too young to be taking part in this night's doings, were grateful to be allowed to look on and listen, so they sank quickly, eagerly, into inconspicuous places near the entrance. Koonooku himself was a famous dance singer. Toozak's eyes immediately found him, taller than most, bright of eye, sitting with the drummers, smiling and joking quietly with them. He knew he was the center of interest, and did not need to raise his voice to attract attention to himself.

Now the women came stooping through the entrance, and there was a low flurry of murmurs, laughter, knowing looks, and they all hurried to one corner, eyes down. The braids were shining and the parkas were new and beautiful, but no sooner had they been seen by all than those parkas must come off, the room was so warm.

The drums began, very low and soft, "toom-toom, toom-toom," and the voices of the seven singers, "Ah, yunga-ah, hunga, ah, ha, ha."

On and on the music went, and the people sat quietly, coming under its spell. Finally Apangalook reached over and touched Pungwi. "It seems to me that I see your partner of last year's festival. How much will you pay this year?"

Laughter from all; the women nudge poor Raganok, who giggles and hides her face. Louder grow the drums and voices. Pungwi looks at the row of old men, the judges, "One white fox skin?"

Ikmallowa smiles. "No more than that? Have you forgotten what a fine dancer the small woman is?" The other old men laugh and nod agreement.

Apangalook murmurs chidingly, "Shame, my neighbor, surely you expect more than a fox skin's worth of pleasure?"

"The fine dancer is also a good maker of skin boots and a fine cook," adds another laughing guest.

So it goes. Pungwi finally offers three skins and rises to meet Raganok in the center of the ningloo. To the fast and yet faster song of the drums they dance, facing each other. When the dance is finished they slip into parkas and quickly crawl out through the passageway.

Wohtillin now nudges Apangalook, "You were so quick to get Pungwi to dancing. What about yourself? I see a certain smooth-skinned woman sitting over there. What will *you* pay?"

"Yes, what will *you* pay?" laughs the chorus. "There is a woman here who is the best sewing woman in Kukulik village and who always has a smile. She also has a new dance to dance this year. What will you do about this?"

This is reason for more laughter and joking among the men, more giggling and hiding of faces among the women. Everyone is having a fine time. Toozak is gazing hard at his father, but he had also noticed someone else. That laughing-eyed Okoma of Yahoh's—how had she gotten here? She was a year younger than he; what business had she at a winter festival? Toozak looked quickly away, but had a sneaking fear that those laughing eyes had caught him. He keeps his eyes on Apangalook now, who is rising. The old men smile, and shake their heads, and then nod and accept Apangalook's payment of three sealskins. He and Mohok of the smiling face, Koonooku's second wife, dance together.

Mohok's new dance is a brisk one of twisting and turning, faster and faster, more and more compelling, till all are singing and swaying, the drummers fairly shrieking with fervor. The performers are shining with exertion. Life is so strong within them they canot possibly express it all. At one point the drums suddenly stop; the dancers and singers continue alone; the drums crash in again, wilder and wilder! Then it is finished, in a breath, in the middle of a beat, and Mohok is standing, smiling and panting, with outflung arms.

Tatoowi leaned close to Toozak. "You notice Yahoh managed to get here. He will be in front of everyone tomorrow when the gifts are given. But tonight," Tatoowi snorted, "tonight I think he will be alone. That wife of his, Anatoonga, is bound to be taken by someone."

Toozak followed Tatoowi's gaze to Anatoonga, sitting across the room, still young and lively and desirable. Of course that brought his gaze across Okoma too, because she sat near her mother. "Too bad," went on the talkative Tatoowi, "that Anatoonga's parents ever betrothed her to that lazy Yahoh. I wonder how he ever paid for her. That must have been hard on his soul."

Anatoonga's face held a sad eagerness, which changed to a complacent glow when one of the chief men of Kukulik began bidding for her dance. Tatoowi again hissed in Toozak's ear, "Look at Yahoh's face now—ha, ha. There is nothing he can do."

But Toozak's eyes, against his will, kept finding the smooth neat figure of Okoma. His mind was unruly, too. It kept pushing forward such thoughts as these: "My parents have not yet betrothed me to anyone. Apangalook would never want to deal with Yahoh, yet Assoonga herself has often said Yahoh's wife and daughter were fine needlewomen and cooks. Smooth skin, and such a small nose she has! And why does she keep glancing this way? Is it Tatoowi or me? Does she think *I* have fox skins already, to spend for a silly girl?"

"Maybe next year," muttered Toozak to himself.

"What is it? What do you say?" inquired that impudent Tatoowi.

"I said—oh, I said nothing," snapped Toozak. "Look there, how did *he* get here?"

Tatoowi looked. "Oh, Walanga. He must have started a day later; he thinks he is different from all other Inuit. It is well for him to travel alone, but why did he want to come?"

Toozak did not answer. "It is too bad Kulukhon was at his trapping camp and could not come with us and be here tonight," he thought.

Seeming to watch Anatoonga, who was just beginning her dance, he saw Walanga's burning eyes roam slowly about the room until they lit upon Tokoya. And in that instant she looked up and met Walanga's eyes. "She looks like a mouse the fox is about to pounce on," thought Toozak. "And Apangalook and Assoonga both gone to other houses to sleep."

On and on went the dance, until every couple had gone to their places, and all the young ones stretched along the back platform in Koonooku's ningloo. Every ningloo in the village was quiet and dark at last.

The lamps in Koonooku's house were burning low. The young boys were already asleep on the rear platform. All but Toozak. He looked at Tatoowi, beside him; Tatoowi might enjoy this, but no, it was better to do it alone. He slid out onto the floor, pulled on all his warm clothes, and stepped over to Tokoya. He leaned over her, and her frightened eyes shone up at him. "Ooh, Toozak," she held his arm tightly, "I thought—"

"Yes, you thought it was that tall fox. Lie still; make no noise. I think if he comes he will not get *this* far!"

Toozak crept out into Koonooku's dark passageway. He was sure he had time. Walanga was smart; he would wait until he was sure all the tired ones were asleep. Toozak was glad Koonooku's passageway was timbered. It made it quite easy to fasten the large baleen noose in the roof and let it hang down to the proper height.

He led the strip of baleen inside the entrance, tied it to his coil of mukluk rope, then curled down in a comfortable position on the floor to wait. From her uneasy rest Tokoya whispered, "Toozak what are you doing?"

"Sh-h—quiet—I am doing nothing now, just waiting. You will see."

Toozak's ear caught the first sound. Someone was crawling, oh, so quietly, through the passageway. One, two, three, four—Toozak waited. Then he peeked around the corner, and pulled.

"Ah, Ahg-gk!" Walanga was lying full length, the noose tight about his neck. Some demon was tying his legs and arms with thong. "Ah, it is too bad," whispered a soft voice. "Birds that flit about in the dark should have eyes to see in the dark, should they not?"

That cursed Toozak! He was too much a man for his years. Walanga's eyes were throbbing, the world was a spinning mass of lights. Did the young devil really mean to finish him off? Ah, a little breath; the horrible thing was loosened a bit, and he heard that laughing young voice whisper again. "It will no doubt be best for you if you lie here very quietly till morning. If you made a noise, people would have to know that you were forcing yourself into places where you were not needed. You perhaps did not understand; my sister does not have to receive anyone she does not *want*."

. . . . .

If anyone missed Walanga next day, it was only for a fleeting moment.

Walanga was not a lovable soul, and soon forgotten, along with all other unpleasant things, in the joy and excitement of festival time. These were the happy days. Nothing must spoil them. Ghosts and wandering souls of departed friends, spirits of storm and famine, were unthought of; gratefully, quickly, they pushed fear to the background and found pleasure in every way they knew. Soon enough perhaps would come sickness or accident or want. Just now they would store up a little happiness. No one was happier than Toozak, even though he was a bit sleepy. He had had to rise very early, to release a prisoner.

Koonooku's gifts were all such as anyone would be glad to accept. Each family had seal skins, walrus meat, frozen fish and frozen auklets to load upon their sleds. And his feast was a rich one. Everyone ate until he was sure he could hold no more.

But then Koonooku's first wife had a surprise for them. She came in from outdoors carrying a large pale green brick, nunivak, fermented in a poke, then frozen. She laid the brick upon a wooden platter and knelt, shaving off very, very thin slices with her oolak, while the whole assembly looked on, mystified. Koonooku smiled proudly, "Sometimes a wife has some new ideas," he observed, watching Asha's quick hands as she poured seal oil from a wooden dish into the platter and began mixing the frosty slices with oil. She was perhaps the smartest of his three wives. She soon had a thick frothy mixture, a green snow-heap, on the platter.

Asha now took a generous pinch of this between her fingers and tossed it quickly into her mouth. The guests all breathed a sigh. They had been wondering how the new food was to be eaten!

There was no doubt Asha's new idea was a good one. In a few moments all were smacking lips loudly and chattering and laughing over this strange and delightful way to use nunivak. And by that time they really were unable to eat another bite. The women of Koonooku's household removed the platters, and on the platforms and on the floor the whole company stretched themselves and rested. They all knew that pretty soon one of the older men would begin the story telling. All were content, and Toozak was so content he was nearly asleep. He and Tatoowi lay in a corner of the platform. Through half-closed eyes he saw Okoma again, not far away, shining braids, shining eyes. It just seemed as though that girl must always be in his eyes. Then through half-conscious ears he heard Ikmallowa begin to speak:

"Here has been festival and joy of men and women; strong men and loving women, proud of youth and strength and the pleasures that go with these. They are not thinking now that someday they will be old, never thinking how sometimes it happens that the old people must be wise for them."

Ikmallowa paused and looked all about the ningloo. It was very quiet. He went on in his soft, slow voice:

So it was with a rich man once.

He and his wife had no children, but he was very good to all children and let them play in his house, and every time gave the children something to eat.

One time his wife went outdoors to empty her trash basket and did not come back. Her husband went out to search in every house and could not find his wife. At last he was very sad and could not sleep for thinking of her, and was still more angry at the children who came to him and sometimes he hurt the children. When he was standing outside he always carried his big knife, and he did not eat, either, for many days.

There was in the village an old woman, who said to her small grandson, "Will you go tell that rich man to come to me?"

The boy said, "No, I do not like to go to him. When I come near him he will kill me. He is very mad because his wife is lost; I have no father to protect me; he will kill me."

Then the old woman said, "You must go and bring him. He will not hurt you if you say like this: 'The old woman wants you to come to her house.' "

Then the boy went, very slowly, to the man's house. When the boy came to him the man said, "Why do you come to me? I will kill you."

The boy cried out, "My grandma sent me because she wants to see you in her house. I was afraid to come here but the old woman says she has to talk to you."

So the man went with the boy and the old woman said to him, *"I have some deer meat that your wife gave me when she was here. Will you eat if I cook it for you?"*

"Yes, I will eat it."

So the man ate the meat and was still hungry. He said to the boy, *"Will you go to my house and bring more deer meat and I will sleep here, too; bring me a deerskin for sleeping."* After the man had eaten more the old woman said, *"Before you go to sleep you have to make a running stick."*

He made it right away and the old woman said, *"Stick the stick in the top of the house so the wind will not bend it."*

And he did so. Then he went to sleep for two days. The third morning he got up and ate some more. Then the old woman said, *"You go out and see the direction the stick is bent. If it is bent, go in that direction. Again when you sleep put the stick in the ground and when you get up follow where it bends always, for if I am right your wife is in that direction."*

The man said, *"All right, I shall go and try."*

He kept on going for many days and when he was sleepy put his stick in the ground and slept. When he got up, he went in the direction the stick was bent. One morning he saw the stick was bent to the ground so he thought he must be near his wife, so he walked very slowly toward a mountain there. When he was part way up the mountain he saw a very big ningloo partly built in the ground, and when he came near it he crept up to the hole in the top and looked in and saw his wife washing the floor. He wondered how he could get her.

He watched till she was under the hole and he spit on her neck. She wiped her neck and looked up and saw her husband. He motioned toward the door. When she finished she said, *"I have a pain in my head; I will go out and empty the pail."*

When she got out the husband said, *"I am coming after you. I am having a very hard time."*

The wife said, *"You could not take me now. Hide somewhere, and I will think of some way."*

When she went in, the big duck, who was the owner of the ningloo, said, *"What! You smell like a man. I think you saw your husband."*

She said, *"You don't know anything. You say my husband is far away. You brought me through the air very fast and you were tired when you got here; no man could come here walking.''*

So they slept but the husband is hiding under the rocks. In the morning when the big duck came out, he smelled a man's smell again, but the woman said, "Last night I washed my husband's charms which I have; maybe that is the smell.'' Then the big duck flew away.

The husband came out from under the rocks and when he went into the big ningloo he saw a big woman and his wife. The big woman said, "Do not kill me. My husband is a bad creature; he does evil in every place. This time I will not help him.''

So the man and his wife traveled homeward for many days, and about half way home they heard a sound of a big duck coming and a voice saying, "If I come to you I will kill you.''

The man and his wife went on and on but finally they came to a river and could not cross and the big duck was coming near. The woman said, "Can you do anything?''

The man said, "Give me a bead.''

And she gave him two beads. He took a bead and breathed on it and threw it on the ground; the bead went in, just like sinking, and the man and woman sunk down with it. The big duck was close to them, and began sweeping the ground with his wing but could not catch them. Then the big duck said, "You stay here. I will do something.''

Then the big duck sat in the river and held all the river's water, so the water began to flood. Then the husband said to his wife, "You had better do something, too.''

She answered, "I will call upon my father's spirit, January.''

And at last the weather began to freeze and the big duck began to freeze onto the river. The man and woman came out of the ground, and the big duck cried, "Little man, do not harm me.''

The man answered, "No, oh no, I will not harm you more than you harmed me,'' and he walked on the ice to the duck and shot him in the eyes with his bow and arrows, so that he was blind.

They went home quickly then, and found the old woman and her grandson, and the man took the boy to be his own and the old woman to be his mother, and kept them always and gave them many good things.

And the man began to play again with the children and give them many good things to eat.

. . . . .

Morning came, and the festival was over. They had been privileged to attend a great festival and they knew there were great men among their people, greatest of all, their generous host. They had broken winter's spell; the festival and the memory of it would speed the long dark days away and spring would come more quickly now, because of Koonooku's festival.

Koonooku was left to start all over again; he had achieved the opportunity of once more building up a great wealth, of holding and proving his place as the best hunter, the wisest and most generous of men, a leader and a benefactor. If he had not given away much of his wealth he would soon have lost that reputation, for all of them must live, and if others had had to beg food and skins from Koonooku he would soon have been hated as a miser and would not have been considered really one of them. But in a joyous festival of giving he had shared everything voluntarily and endeared himself to all. With contented souls, he and Raganok and Mohok and Asha stood before their big house and bade their guests good-bye till summer.

They watched team after team bound away over the low hummocks and disappear into the gray fog.

CHAPTER VII

Magic Lamp Bowl

WIND AND SNOW came howling down the day after the people left for the festival, but Sekwo and Notangi were safe and warm in the house at home, with old Yokho, and in the passageway were oil and meat and a poke of greens. They need not go outside till the storm went away.

Sekwo and Notangi sat before the big lamp and peered into its drip bowl. "Yokho, the bowl is soon full of oil. Do you think it time for small girls to have some gum to chew?"

Yokho looked up from the polar bear hunting pants she was making for Apangalook and smiled at those two round, hopeful faces. She came and knelt beside the children and looked under the lamp. "Yes, perhaps—"

She lifted the lamp itself and set it aside, then took the clay drip bowl out into the passageway, the little girls at her heels. From under one of the sleeping platforms she pulled some fine dry kindlings of willow root and kindled them at the smaller lamp. Out in the passageway again, she laid the flaming torch in the drip bowl, and there was a mighty flame.

"Children have gum now, when we have good times and many seals," she said, watching the light flickering over the two pleased faces. "If it were hard times, small children might not have gum, for the oil would have to be used over again in the lamp. I have seen it so—ay-yah."

Yokho seemed to go far away, gazing into the flame as though she saw scenes from long ago. Suddenly she smiled and laid her hand on Sekwo's shoulder. "It is burning low now. We can take it inside." They all sat on the floor, the flaming bowl before them. "Did you know that a lamp drip-bowl was once magic?" asked Yokho.

Now the little girls knew there was a story coming, and they curled up close together, eyes still watching the wonderful flame, so much more of a flame than an ordinary lamp. How quiet it was in the ningloo! Only the wind's song, surging back and forth over the roof out there.

Once there was a lucky man. He caught a whale every spring. But he did not good worship to the whale's spirit. He hung the flukes for many days and let them dry. In the winter he sent the whale's spirit in the flukes to heaven but the spirits then are too tired to stay there; they had been dried too long. Next time the lucky man did the same wrong way.

In the evening his son went outside and heard the sound of walrus very close to the shore. He went to try to catch it but the walrus is going farther all time, but he keep on trying it. And the boy never thought, and kept on trying. He went far from shore on the ice. While he was trying to catch a walrus he knew he was far from the shore. Then the wind began to blow from the north very hard, and the wind carry him away very far from shore. Soon he got no place, the ice broke and there was no place for him to sit down; he stood on the ice and the water came halfway to his waist. He thought and thought. At last he thought he must kill himself, because he was having a hard time. Soon he warmed his knife to use on himself. While he was warming his knife, he heard a voice of a man in the air and it said, "Don't kill yourself. Don't dare it."

Then he put away his knife, and thought for a long time, and then he thought, "This time I will really use my knife."

Then he warmed it again, and the voice spoke again and said, "Come on, I will take you up to heaven and save you."

Then he put away his knife again and saw a man who said, "Come on and put your hand on my back and close your eyes," and the young man did so, and they started walking, and there was a sound like going up in the air, and then the man said, "Open your eyes and see."

The boy opened his eyes but could not see at first, it was so bright. After a while he saw five houses. Then he went to the first house and the man said, "I found a boy which was a whale-killing man's son. Will you take care of him?"

Then the man inside said, "We do not know how to care for him. Take him to the second house."

And he did so and the man in the second house said, "No, I will not take care of him. Take him to the third house."

And he tried the third and fourth houses and it was the same. Finally he went to the fifth house and the man inside said, "Who is that?"

And the man said, *"I found a boy that was a son of a whale-killing man. Will you take care of him?"*

Then the fifth house man said, *"Stay here. I will take care of him."* And he was pounding inside the house, and came out with a strong box that fitted to the body of a man. He put the boy in the box and gave him a little to eat and a little to drink on the first day, and on the second day less food and water. And the third and fourth days less and less and kept on doing that way and the boy became very thin.

Now the father was in great sorrow for his son. He sent after every Singer to come to him because he wanted his son to come back. His wife said to him, *"You, why did you kill so many whales?"*

Her husband said, *"Make the sacrificial food for me."*

She did this and in the evening he took his paddle and said to his wife, *"Follow me with the dish of food."*

Then they began to go to the shore and he said to his wife, *"When I go into the water you put this holy food in the water after me and sing a song of the whaleboats."*

So he went into the water and asked the people of the sea, *"Did you see my boy?"*

The people of the sea said, *"I do not know."* But he kept on asking and someone said, *"I heard that up in heaven there is a boy that came from here and that was a son of a whale-killing man."*

Then the people of the sea took the father up to heaven and when he came to the fifth house he said, *"Will you please let my son come to me?"*

The man of the fifth house said, *"No, you cannot see your boy because you were not good to the whale I sent to you."*

Now there was a face in the man's paddle and it began to speak and said, *"Say to him you have a dog you will give to him."*

So the man said, *"I have a dog I will give to you if you will let me see my son."*

The man in the house let him see his son, and he saw how poor and thin he was. The father went back down to his village and told his wife he saw their son and he was very thin.

In this village there was an old woman and a granddaughter living in a little ningloo. The little girl said to herself, *"How can the little lost boy come back again?"*

Then the little girl heard a voice which said, *"The lamp-drip bowl will save a boy."*

The little girl took the drip pot outside and watched. It began to move around in the fire. While it was moving around it began to jump, and jumped up to heaven, and went to the boy's cage, and everybody there watched it. Then the man in the house said, "Why have they sent this thing that is no good for anything?"

But the drip-bowl kept on jumping around in the fire, and finally it began to catch the boy, and took him, and brought him down to the little girl's ningloo. Then the girl went to the boy's father and asked, "Can we use some of your boy's clothes? Maybe nobody would use them now."

The father was willing and the girl took them home. The boy put on his clothes and went to his father and mother, and they were very much surprised and asked, "Who brought you back to us?"

The boy answered, "The little girl brought me back."

And the father said, "Now we will help and take care of her and her grandmother, too. Now, my son, you will be her husband and she will be your wife."

Yokho stopped. Sekwo and Notangi were both bent curiously over the drip bowl, and with the bone lamp tool Sekwo was carefully pulling out some fine thick black gum.

"Up onto the platform now, both of you," cried Yokho, "while I fix this lamp and cook us some broth—whoosh!" And she held her fingers like tusks at the side of her chin and, like a big walrus, chased the two squealing ones up onto the sleeping robes.

There they rolled like two pup seals, and chewed the delicious gum, while old Yokho was very busy about the cooking. No one here to interfere with her now. She hummed a little song as she stirred the broth. Much better than going to a festival two whole sleeps away through snow and cold!

·TAHEGLOKHSEK·
Moon of Appearing of Mukluk,
Young Big Seal

CHAPTER VIII

Toozak and Kaka

"A VERY FINE DAY for one to try to catch his first big seal," growled Toozak at Kaka through stiff lips. "If you can do so, you are a real hunter."

The wind picked up a cloud of snow and hurled it into Toozak's face. He pushed his shoulders into the storm, bent nearly double. His young friend had been so determined to go out this day, and he, Toozak, the always-good-natured one, had given him his way.

Kaka was smiling. He tested his harpoon, raising it over his head as though to cast it, bracing his short legs to keep the shaft from sailing out into the wind. "There are few fine days for hunters, Ikmallowa says. It is as well I start out on a bad one. Pungwi has said I have had enough of the exercises for boys to be strong now."

Toozak only muttered; he thought they would never come to the heaped rough ice at the edge of the shore ice, though on a fine day it was no distance at all. They began clambering up over the jumbled cakes, slipping back, pulling themselves up again. When they reached the top Toozak shouted, "Kehh, this wind! I wonder if it cannot sometimes be tired of blowing."

Wind and snow were tearing at them; the fur of their hoods was blown into their mouths; their eyelashes were hung with frost. A terrible day, but Kaka was determined. He pushed the fur out of his face and looked eagerly out over the pack, touched Toozak's arm, and pointed.

Far out there between swirling clouds was a dark something. Toozak looked, pushed the fur out of his eyes, looked again. "Mukluk it is! And no other hunters out this day to hear your call, if you get him. He will be all yours. Go ahead, if you still think you can."

They both crouched, and Kaka began the slow advance toward his first big catch. He crawled rapidly, eyes on the seal. Mukluk was taking a nap on the ice; a good-sized one he was, a Nughsopek, lying full length, unmindful of the wind or the fine frosty snow blowing over him. Kaka crawled and crawled, being careful not to let his spear scratch the ice and make a sharp sound. Even though the wind howled, Nughsopek had ears.

When Nughsopek raised his head every minute or so to look about, Kaka was instantly motionless. Nughsopek slept again; Kaka crawled. He was getting fairly near now. Toozak now crouched behind an ice hummock out of the wind, watching the hunt, enjoying it.

Nughsopek slept again; Kaka crawled. Nughsopek raised his head; Kaka was an immovable lump. Nughsopek gazed curiously at this lump. Kaka, with the ivory seal scratcher he carried in one hand, scratched on the ice. Nughsopek lay down again; evidently the lump was only another seal.

But suddenly Nughsopek felt a sudden shock, a flaming pain, and Kaka stood with spear imbedded in his first seal!

Now Toozak came running with his baleen toboggan, forgetting the storm. "It looks as though there might be one more hunter on Sevuokuk," he laughed. "Now you can learn the proper way to take your catch home."

Toozak laid Nughsopek on the toboggan, on his back, his head upon the rolled-up baleen strip at the front. His flippers he crossed upon his breast and tied, and his body was lashed criss-cross with mukluk rope, pulled through the lashing loops along both sides of the toboggan.

Now Kaka's big catch was ready, and they turned gladly enough homeward. The storm had become a blizzard, choking them with flying snow, pushing against them like a great unseen hand, soft yet all-powerful.

So Kaka came to his father's house, and stood outside and shouted, "Is there a woman to receive a seal?"

Walla came hurrying with the bowl of water, her eyes proud, for her son had gotten for his first big catch, not just a seal, but a big mukluk, Nughsopek. When the seal spirit had been pleased with water, the big seal was carried in and laid in the center of the house.

Pungwi now hurried to Apangalook's house and came back with old Ikmallowa. While Pungwi and Walla and Ega all looked on smilingly, the old man led Kaka to the seal and knocked him down; right across the seal he fell. When he rose, Ikmallowa led him around to the other side of the seal and knocked him down again. While Kaka lay there across the seal, Ikmallowa lifted his face and prayed aloud to the spirits of animals to give Kaka good fortune in all his hunting days.

Kaka rose. His father pointed to the small urine tub which stood empty under the platform. Kaka took the tub, went out of the house and over to the refuse pile at one side. Here with elaborate motion he pretended to empty the tub. He had performed a woman's job for the first and last time. He had now become a hunter.

In the house, Pungwi held out to Ikmallowa a fine new snowshirt. "An insignificant thanks for your help in making this young boy into a hunter."

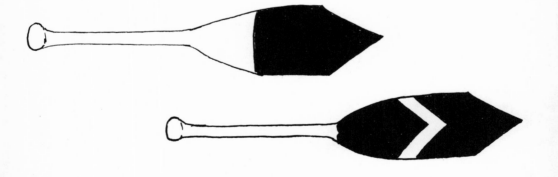

· HOGHVEK ·
Moon for Using Bird Slings

CHAPTER IX

Toozak the Trapper

EASTWARD over the black inland peaks the sky was gold; the sun was coming earlier these days; winter's blackest hours had passed by once more.

Before Pungwi's house, the dogs in their sealskin harnesses were yelping to be gone. Toozak and Timkaroo, big and shaggy in their dogskin hunting pants, flung themselves onto the sled. Away through the village, across the gravel spit, over the steep bank, almost flying, onto the hard trail across the lake, and around the eastern side of the Cape Mountain they sped. Cold it was, but there was light in the world again, and dogs and men all felt life surging up in them to defy the darkness and welcome the light. One could almost think of spring and whaling.

Toozak thought of the many times during that long winter he had come out over this familiar way, often in darkness of early morning or early evening, in days when the sun only peered at Sevuokuk and was gone again, often by moonlight, so bright, so bitter cold. Sometimes when the lights bloomed in the northern sky, running by the sled, frost hung all over his furs, sticking his eyelashes together—up little steep valleys, over the boulder-strewn beds of summer's rushing little streams, around the shoulders of all the little hills. He knew so well every rock, every giant boulder, every dip and hollow. In cold and hunger, with good catch or none, often alone, he had traveled these, the trapping grounds of the family of Apangalook.

He turned in his seat to look at his tall brother. "Are you thinking, Timkaroo, that it is good to have some sunlight to travel by? See there, once in a while she can stick her face through the fog, to make us feel better. Then this wind does not feel quite so bad."

"Some people think," answered Timkaroo, "that if we young men take enough exercise we will never feel the cold, but perhaps those people have never been out all day long on the ice, or following a trap line. Dogskin pants feel pretty good today, even though we do see the sun sometimes. Ah-hk, Tootu, you will try to bite your partner's heels again?"

Timkaroo uncoiled his mukluk whip; he had a strip of beluga skin at its tip which made a fine sharp crack when he snapped it in front of the cranky Tootu. "Tootu is like the old-time people of Miyowaghameet, starting to fight in the morning."

"Those were the people whose old village we can still see at the foot of the mountain there. Why did they fight?"

Timkaroo stopped the dogs in the lee of a great jumble of rocks and, still flicking the whip about, sat on the front of the sled. The dogs, panting and peaceful for a moment, sat quietly on their haunches, red tongues lolling. "No one knows why those two long-ago villages fought. Sevuokuk people nowadays do not think of such things."

Timkaroo chuckled. "It was so very long ago; perhaps they were a different kind of people, from a different part of the country over the water. In the morning the Miyowaghameet would come out with bows and arrows and start shooting at the neighbors in Ievoghiyogameet, because in the morning the sun shone toward Ievoghiyogameet, and those people could not see to shoot. So they shot until all the arrows were gone and then started with spears until they got tired. Then in the evening, when the sun shone on Miyowaghameet, the Ievoghiyogameet started, and they had the same thing all over again."

Toozak laughed. "They had a fine plan to kill each other all away. With so much fighting there could not be much hunting. I am not surprised that both villages have been empty and cold for a long, long time."

The boys both looked back down over the slopes to two snowy hummocks on the other side of the lake, the two warlike villages, snow-covered in winter and grass-covered in summer, empty of life, filled with spirits; no one went near. Toozak suddenly wondered if Walanga might not be descended from these contrary old inhabitants. He had stayed out of the way since the night of the festival at Kukulik, yet Toozak was not quite easy in his mind.

Timkaroo whistled. The dogs were off like arrows shot from bows. Tootu tried to give the dog ahead of him a nip in the heels, but could not quite reach. They were soon pulling up to the pile of boulders where they had set their first trap.

"Ah, the spirits are kind today. We have a fox in the first trap!" Timkaroo lifted the beautiful white body from the shallow pit. The fox was already dead.

Toozak could see the story: a hungry fox, sniffing about boulder piles for a mouse hole. In a shallow pit under a whale vertebra, carved out big enough to allow a fox's head to slip easily through its center, there was a delicious smell—ptarmigan! The prowling fox had thrust his head through the opening and in so doing, brought about his neck the noose of baleen, so cleverly made, so cleverly laid about the hole by Inuit who also liked to live, and to have warm white fur for their babies.

The next trap was not far away, but here they had used a different scheme, a piece of whale rib to which they had fastened a spring of twisted sinew. At the end of the sinew spring there was a stick of wood, in which were fastened three sharp pieces of bone. This trap had been sprung. Some animal had had some kind of trouble here; fox tracks led away up the slope. Toozak followed them, up over a little hill, down around an overhanging rock to a jumble of shale on the hillside, where lay, not the white fox they were accustomed to catch, but a red one. Toozak did not touch the dead animal. He shouted, and Timkaroo came running.

"Ah, ah, Kovvepek, eh? You did not touch him? " He looked sharply at Toozak.

"Touch him!" Toozak's eyes were round. "I have not trapped very long, but I know that to pick up a white fox dead without a wound is bad luck, and that to take a red one without a wound is far worse. Do I want harm for myself and my family for generations to come? But, I am sure it was a blow from our stick trap which took him. Look."

He bent over the fox and pointed to his head, where a bloody stain showed. There could be no doubt Kovvepek had wounds.

So without fear, they lifted him and carried him back to the sled.

As they slid down into the next little valley, Timkaroo pointed. "See there, where the valley is very narrow, I think we can have our fox drive. We can stretch the sinew net across there, in that narrow place."

"Oh yes, and all of us will have plenty of exercise," laughed Toozak, "driving foxes from all these slopes down into that net! We have to both run and shout, plenty of exercise. Apangalook will have to feed us all pretty well at the end of *that* day!"

The fox drive was always a day of pleasure, much work but great fun, and great eating afterward.

On top of the next ridge they stopped. This was the limit of their trapping grounds. Timkaroo pointed, "There goes Walanga; he has looked at his last trap."

Some tall person, all alone with pack on back, was disappearing around the big rock jumble across the hollow. Toozak thought he could see him turn and look back, then he went on without a sign. "Anyone else among our people would have lifted an arm in greeting," growled Timkaroo, "Walanga is like the flesh-eating walrus of the pink tusks—always alone."

Five foxes lay on the sled, but hunger and cold had crept into the trappers before they could at last turn homeward and drive into the very last sunlight. The wind had died. It was quiet and very cold; only the snowy slopes looked warm at last, brushed with live color from the western sky. Down these slopes the dogs ran, knowing they were nearly home; maybe they were thinking of fresh seal meat, just as Toozak was.

At the edge of the village they met three young boys. This was the moon of bird slinging. One of the boys was Kaka, and he proudly held up a big snowy owl. "Oh, ho," laughed Timkaroo, "Anneepa they have snared this day. I think some hopping is to take place."

Toozak remembered very well that ceremony of the snowy owl. Times enough he had done it, before he came to this season of being a man. The owl would be hung head down from the center post and the lamp placed underneath. Then the boys would hop around the lamp sideways, side by side, hop and hop until they were all tired out. Suddenly, they would snatch the owl and begin pulling out the spotted wing feathers, all trying to get the head or the feet. Finally, two boys would triumphantly hold the feet, and these they would take home. Siyak, the small boys' ceremony of Anneepa, would be over.

"I think they will be too tired when it is over to eat the meat tonight."

"Oh no, when their mother has it all boiled, they will manage to be awake enough to eat, and I should like to be there to help them," laughed Toozak. He could almost taste the delicate flavor of boiled owl, like deer meat from over the water. And the added delicacy of the rendered-out fat from Anneepa mixed with snow to a fluffy white mass—oh, that was too much for a hungry fox trapper to think of! He was glad they were rushing through the village and almost home!

Timkaroo left him and his share of the foxes at the door of their father's house and drove the dogs on toward the house of Pungwi, his future father-in-law. *His,* Timkaroo's, share of foxes would go to Pungwi, part of the payment for that smiling Ega. Toozak stood and watched Timkaroo drive away, then swiftly he walked back through the village the way they had just come. Surely he had been given sharp eyes for some use, and his curiosity was stronger then his hunger right now.

At the corner of Massiu's house he stopped. No one in sight. He crept carefully to the corner, peered around. Yes, there they were, under Massiu's meat rack, Walanga and that fat young Kooungo from Kukulik, who had come back from the festival with Massiu's mother for a visit.

In the dusk the two were one, noses pressed together in a long kiss. Toozak grinned, then spat. "So—that bold-eyed one! She is a good match for a long, hungry, flesh-eating walrus. Perhaps we shall have peace now."

The two were still there under the meat rack as Toozak slipped away. His curiosity was satisfied and hunger was shouting within him.

Back at home, he dragged his foxes into the entrance and piled them by the door; when they had had their evening meal, they would all start skinning. Afterward, he would carry the carcasses out and put them high on the meat rack where the dogs could not reach them.

Assoonga looked up from a steaming pot of meat. "Ah, young one, your sacrifices must have pleased the Maker of Foxes."

She hurried forward to take his clothes off for him. He smiled and leaned to whisper in her ear. "Think you I shall be able to earn a wife some day?"

His mother made a smiling face at him, opening her eyes wide in her round face, said nothing, carried his clothes to the drying rack. Ah, this Toozak of hers, he was one to be loved by all; she, his mother, would never be able to show all her love for him.

Toozak stretched his naked body in the warmth of the sleeping platform. After the long day, the miles of running through icy air, how good this felt! He thought of the words, "Maker of Foxes." Yes, he had done his best; so had Timkaroo. It was Apangalook's training. Before they had set their first trap in the fall they had saved the proper things for a sacrifice. On a certain morning in October they had risen very early and placed these things in a platter—codfish, sculpin, auklets, all torn to tiny pieces. With the proper words and in all earnestness they had tossed these pieces into the air, giving them to the Maker of Foxes.

Now he lay in comfort after a good day's catch and through half-closed eyes watched Assoonga stir that delicious-smelling food over the lamp. The spirits must be friendly toward him; he had become a trapper now as well as a hunter.

When the season was over they would do a proper ceremony again. Early some morning soon the carcasses would all have to be brought in and piled by the center post and by them a lamp set, and the sacrificial food brought in. Toozak could see them there, he and Timkaroo, tossing bits of seal liver to the carcasses, to the air, to the Maker of Foxes, and then cutting off all the fox heads and legs, carrying them in a bag far out behind the village. And yes, before he left them on the tundra, he would not forget to speak softly to those heads and legs and ask them to bring him more good luck in future. Animals were so much like people; their souls must be forever thought of and pleased.

Pleased—"Yes," Toozak was thinking drowsily, "people liked to be pleased too." Someday, someone would have to please *him,* too, someone quick and shining-eyed, someone with color of tundra flowers in her cheeks, and such a small enticing nose!

CHAPTER X

Iviek Again

APANGALOOK brought the ungiak up against the ice floe so quietly that the big female walrus dozing there heard nothing. Toozak dug his paddle-point into the ice and watched Kulukhon leap onto the floe and run, crouching. The baby Iviek, curled beside his mother, looked sleepily at a strange thing coming toward him. His mother turned, and received Kulukhon's harpoon in her neck.

Toozak gripped his paddle harder and shivered. Before mother Iviek could push herself to the water's edge, Kulukhon had struck with his spear. Toozak heard Apangalook call from the stern of the boat, "Get her baby too; it is the law. Without any mother's milk this little one might grow to be a flesh-eating walrus that eats seals, and sometimes men, too."

Mother Iviek's terrible roar rose to a scream, and stopped. She rolled over, gasping; the echo of that sound spread over the ice floes, was answered by grunts and sudden movements among the rest of the herd, a mass of black bodies at the other end of the floe. The hunters stood back, watching her death struggles. Toozak still crouched in the boat but he could not take his eyes away. Mortally wounded she was. Suddenly from the blow-hole in top of her skull the blood rose, a red fountain against the blue spring sky. Bloody spray shot out over the whiteness of ice and snow and over the hunters. Mother Iviek sank into a lifeless black heap. Toozak shivered again. He probably wasn't a real hunter yet.

Baby Iviek crawled to his mother, crawled upon her warm body, nuzzled for food. Kulukhon advanced with his spear. It was the law.

But Toozak looked away to the other end of the big floe. The other crews were having a lively enough time, trying to harpoon some walrus on the ice before they got into the water. Even Yahoh was hopping about at a great

77

speed for him. Grunts that rose to roars, and a great heaving, pushing mass of black hulks moving toward the water. The hunters had an advantage, for those mothers who had young were loath to leave them, and were having trouble shoving their babies into the water.

Toozak watched a baby sleeping on the ice. Its mother slid into the water. Baby still slept. Mother swam back and held onto the ice with her front flippers, grunting and talking to her sleepy child. No, he would not move. She raised herself further, reached her flippers about her ignorant child and pulled him down with her. Toozak twisted about in his seat to watch her go swimming swiftly far out into the blue water, baby riding calmly on her back, his little flippers turned into suction cups to keep him on. Toozak laughed aloud and waved his paddle. "Swim fast, smart one; you deserve to get away from all the hunters."

. . . . .

Home after the hunt—there was a busy village! Before each boat, all along the beach, were piles of slabs of mangona, and before these piles, all the crews, working furiously.

Timkaroo and Toozak worked together. Toozak hauled a slab over quickly to Timkaroo; he hoped he could show him that he was old enough for *this* work, too. Timkaroo swiftly cut a narrow strip off around the edges of the slab, leaving it still attached at one corner, then rolled his end toward Toozak, tucking the ends in neatly. Now, nothing but skin was showing. "Hold now, Toozak, while I sew this."

He made quick slashes through both edges with his stone blade, pulled the end of the narrow strip of skin and meat through, laced it back and forth all across the edge of the big roll, and fastened the end. One more slab ready for the meat cellar, and in the cellar, meat and blubber, inside the skin cover, would keep a long time and take on a fine flavor.

Toozak was already reaching for another slab; they were going to be a fast pair! They laughed, and puffed, and hurried, and this part was much better than the slaughter on the floes. Dogs licked the scraps of meat and blubber, and children ran chattering from group to group, comparing the loads of each boat and looking at all the heads. They got in the way of the workers, but no one rebuked them; children were such precious things, they should do as they liked.

Toozak breathed deeply and wiped the sweat from his face. It hadn't been so very long since *he* had had nothing to do but run around and see what fun he could find. Timkaroo was willing to stop a moment, too, and see what the rest of them were doing. "Busy village today," he laughed. "Even our lone fox is working with other people."

Yes, so he was; Walanga was there, working under his father Ozook's meat rack. He was even smiling—smiling at that plump one from Kukulik who worked beside him. Perhaps he had at last forgotten the family of Apangalook.

All over the village, meat was either going into cellars or being dragged up to them from the beach, already sewed, or being cut into strips and hung to dry. Into the misty, mild air of April rose a hum of talk and laughter. Assoonga and Tokoya, under Apangalook's meat rack, were lifting long strips of meat onto the rack with poles.

On a big rock at one side sat old Yokho and she was happy. She was working on the long coil of walrus small intestine. It would someday make a fine rain shirt for one of their men. Okoma sat close by. She was learning from Yokho, very attentive. From this spot she could also get quick glances toward the cellar where Toozak was now throwing in slabs.

With her thumb nail Yokho pulled off the fatty membrane. This she put into a wooden tray at her side; it would boil up into a fine meal, with greens. Now she had Sekwo and little Notangi both working too, helping her turn all the intestine wrong side out. This inside must be scraped too; the scrapings went into the tray. The two little girls and Okoma crouched and watched. Yokho sang little scraps of song, "Ah, ah, yunga, ah," in her high old voice, and the scraping went on swiftly.

Now came Tokoya, smiling, with a big bowl of water, and helped them wash out the long coil. Tokoya hummed as she worked, too, and Okoma knew why. Tokoya *should* hum; she was young and strong and well-loved by a young hunter of recognized ability; she was also the daughter of one of the leaders of the people. Her place in the world was really to be envied. "And yes," thought Toozak, listening to her song, "that other one has not been near you since the days at Kukulik—that is another reason for singing. It looks as though the Kukulik girl is enough."

Tokoya's strong little hands flashed up and down in the bowl of water; the scum and bits of loose meat and fat from the intestines rose to the surface. Off she strode, still humming, for more water. The faster this was done the better. It was too late in the season to dry the intestines by freezing. This coil would have to be sun dried, and so would be transparent, but it would make good raincoats. Tokoya called to Sekwo, "Come, girl, and bring the others. We are going to have some fun now."

The intestine was clean, the water on it clear. Yokho knotted a piece of baleen around one end, and at the other end, Tokoya and Okoma crouched and took turns blowing. Here was the hard part, for those children all stood there in a row holding the long tube over their arms and laughing, and beyond them Toozak and Kulukhon and all the rest of the workers took time to watch, and laugh at them, and shout all kinds of good advice. How could Yokho expect them to keep on blowing?

But at last the children held a long smooth tube, and the two girls, breathing hard and laughing, too, now, folded it back and forth in big loops, tied it in the middle, and fastened it to a corner of the meat rack to dry. When it was all dry and transparent they could take it down and cut it all along its length, making it into a roll of transparent leather for clothing that would turn away all rain and mist.

Toozak and Timkaroo tossed the last slab of meat into the cellar, covered the opening with the shoulder blade of a whale, then with sod and rocks. They strolled over to Pungwi's house. Outside the house on a flat rock sat Pungwi, and opposite him, on a stool of whale vertebra, there was Yahoh. They were making rope. The big skin of a female walrus had been soaking many days in water, and the outer skin with the hair on it had sloughed off. The big wet hide was spread between the two men. Yahoh held the edge, pulling on it, while Pungwi cut. Pungwi smiled as he worked, for he was doing something he liked to do. He was the best rope maker in the village. He held his left thumb over the edge of the skin measuring the width of the rope, and at the end of his thumb, as it moved along, moved his sharp stone knife, held in his right hand.

Round and round the hide they went, and the pile of inch-wide walrus ribbon behind Yahoh grew. Pleasant work, this. The crews who had finished putting meat away came and joined Toozak and Timkaroo on the ground, and watched the rope making. "This is work Yahoh is best at," whispered Toozak to Timkaroo, "sitting down and looking important."

Yahoh's fat face was creased with satisfied smiles. He held up to Ikmallowa a piece of the walrus hide which held an old scar. Ikmallowa smiled, too. "Perhaps this was one Agnaya sewed together when she dwelt among Iviek."

"Agnaya?" asked Toozak. "Who was she?"

Everyone was quiet now. Toozak looked around the circle of older men. They were all watching his grandfather, and he realized there was a story coming. Ikmallowa was making a paddle, and he kept on shaping it cleverly with his old stone knife while he spoke.

There was once a man whose name was Oghehlowak. His wife's name was Agnaya and she was one of the Owaleet tribe women. She had one child who was a boy just beginning to walk. One fall it was windy with the south wind blowing and the waves high. Oghehlowak was angry at his wife and frightened her out. With her child she walked toward the seashore. When she was almost at the edge of the sea the neighbors called to her husband that she was going into the sea. He ran after her but before he reached her she was in the water walking and carrying her child on her neck.

When she had passed the breakers she found herself on dry land. She walked on and on and came to a bank. She climbed the bank. When she came beyond it, she found it was full of all kinds of seaweed with which she and the child satisfied their hunger. She walked again and came to another bank where she found clams and other shell fish and stopped there and ate all she wanted.

After traveling for some time, she came to a house and entered and found some people with large eyes and short extremities. They were very hospitable. They brought in a platter of tom cod which the woman and her child ate. They stayed there for several days and had the same kind of food every day, of which she tired.

One day, she and her child went on and came to another house where the people were the same as those in the first house, only they were taller. In this house they ate clams and crabs. They stayed there for several days again. From these people she learned about the first people. They were hair seals who changed their forms to that of human beings.

After several days she continued her journey and came to a large entrance of a ningloo. In it she saw a pile of walrus heads with tusks. Some of the heads had only one tusk while some had broken ones. When she entered, clams were served on a wooden platter. She and her child stayed there for a long time, and they received much kindness.

One morning the young men of the house prepared to go out. One said he would go to the one who had the best walrus line. The other said he would be with a person who had a poor line. Another said he would be with a person with a poor harpoon head. When they were in the entrance where the heads were, they each got a head and put it on and turned into walrus and swam off.

In the evening they came home, some with walrus line harpoon heads which the people had harpooned and then lost. The ones who had said they would be with the best weapons did not come home. They had been killed. When they came in with harpoon heads or lines she, Agnaya, cut off the piece pierced and sewed the place up which would heal in a few days. The piece which she cut off from the skin was boiled and eaten by herself and the child. When the wounds healed in a few days they said she was a good magician.

She stayed there a long time and became well acquainted with them. But one day she wished to travel a little further. One morning she and her child went on their journey. About evening she came to a much larger entrance than the others were. When she looked in, she saw a pile of whale flukes, some large and some small. When she entered, there was an old man who never went out.

She stayed there many days with these people. One day the old man asked her if she were homesick. She told him she was, but did not know the way back to her home. The old man told one of the youngest men in the house to take her on the following morning.

The next morning the young man who had been appointed by the old man clothed himself with whale skin. He was no longer a human being but a calf whale. Agnaya and her child sat on his back and the whale swam toward land. The whale swam near Sevuokuk Village.

It was a good day for hunting in the canoe. When the whale was sighted the boats went out to watch. The whale with the woman and child was under the water watching up. The boats which were not successful hunters were as black as ravens whose shadows reach the bottom of the sea. Some came along whose shadows were not as black as these. They were between the poor and the good hunters. At last a boat came which had no shadow. The woman could see it faintly above them. When they came near the whale wanted to take a breath, but the woman kept him from going up. As they waited down there, the woman heard the captain of the boat pray to the spirit of the whale, which made him restless. He asked the woman to let him get a breath but she would not.

At last she could not keep him down any longer. He went up and took his breath near the boat. The boat paddled toward it and struck it. When the whale pulled down the pokes, the woman cut the lines, leaving one poke with the whale. When she cut the line, the other two pokes floated up on the water. When the boat came to the pokes and pulled the line up, they found the line had been broken. It looked as if it had been cut with a knife. So the boat lost the whale and one poke.

When the line was cut, the woman cut off a large piece of the whale skin with large whaling harpoon head, and sewed the place where the harpoon head was.

Then the whale swam with the woman and child toward a place a little south of here, and landed them. When they came on land the woman carried the poke and line on her back and walked toward the village. When she and the child came near the village, she saw a man working at his boat rack. The man was one of the Ahlngoghak tribe and was the best whaler. As she came near him, he looked at them eagerly, for he recognized her. She was the one who had walked into the sea in the fall. The time when she came home was spring. When she and the child reached the man, he saw his whale line and the poke which he had lost that same day.

He did not ask her where she came from, but asked her where she had got the line. She told him she found it on the shore where it had drifted in. He then told her that he had lost a whale with a line and had noticed the line had been cut off with a knife.

When she arrived at the village, she did not go to her husband's house but went to her own people, the Owalek tribe.

Afterward, when her child grew up to be a man, he was the most successful hunter and killed many walrus every winter. From that time the Owalek tribe were the best walrus hunters of the village. When a member of this tribe approached a herd of walrus, they were not afraid, and the walrus were never afraid of them.

It is told that one of their men became a walrus. The female walrus are around the island in fall but go south where the open water is. When these walrus were going south one fall, the man went with them and came back in spring with them on the last ice. He stayed with his people only in summer and left in the fall. He did this for many years until at last walrus hair began to grow on his body. When his body was almost covered with walrus hair, he told his people he would no longer be with them but would stay away with the walrus, forever. He did not come back any more. After that he was seen among the herd of walrus for several springs.

Once while he was staying with his people, he taught them a ceremony which the walrus had taught him to hold in the fall, which would bring the walrus near the island. This ceremony is called "Taghekhsek" which means, calling in the walrus. This is done only by the men of the Owalek tribe.

"So that is why Pungwi, here, is such a good walrus hunter," finished Ikmallowa. "His family is of the Owalek tribe."

"A great rope maker, too," laughed Timkaroo, pointing at the pile of smooth wet ribbon. "Come, Toozak, let us wind the rope for Pungwi."

Away they went, laughing and staggering under the great slippery mass dragging between them. Between two posts they began to wind the rope back and forth, back and forth, forty feet up and forty feet back, pulling the wet stuff a little. "The sun and wind will finish this work," said Toozak, tying the end tight. "Pungwi will have a good new coil of big rope for whaling this year."

At last, only the dogs were there, sniffing and licking about the place where all the rope making, leather making, meat cutting, had been going on. Darkness had come, and with it a cold wind, rolling cold mist in again over the island. The women had all gone in, to prepare plenty of food.

Toozak was weary, but after all, it was not so bad to walk home with the men, not bad at all to be received with swift attention by the women. He stood dreamily just inside the doorway while Assoonga tugged at his parkas, yet his eyes, those sharp eyes, were not asleep. He saw Kulukhon look directly at Tokoya, "We have had a good day among the floes and at the meat cellars, but hunters now come looking for comfort."

Tokoya was smiling at Kulukhon and came swiftly forward and pulled off his parka for him. "Soon there will be food for the hunters." She spoke softly, to him alone, gazing right into his eyes.

Toozak sighed. They were really married, then. By speaking openly to each other in the presence of all the family, they had announced it. Well, he was glad to see that some people could smile. His own lips were stiff with weariness.

In another year perhaps he would not get so numb and tired. In another year—the face, the quick bright eyes of that Okoma came to him again. She had been somewhere near him it seemed, all the day out there. She always had that little smile—Toozak was almost asleep; the moment the ceremony of the walrus heads was over, he tumbled onto the sleeping platform. Assoonga came and pulled his boots off and he lay there, letting waves of warm odors and warm air pour over him.

As in a half dream he heard the family life going on; Tokoya and Kulukhon talking low and chuckling together as she knelt and untied his boot strings; Assoonga instructing Sekwo about getting sour greens out of the poke for the meat; his father telling Yokho about the numbers of Iviek brought into the village that day. It had been a great day. Then he heard his grandmother say, "Do not let your youngest hunter go to sleep there without food; hunters must eat well."

That was it! He was hungry! And he was able to move his numb legs off the platform all right when Assoonga came with the platter. Boiled seal meat, boiled braided intestines, with nunivak, and fresh mangona. That put new blood in one's body! The right ending for a great day.

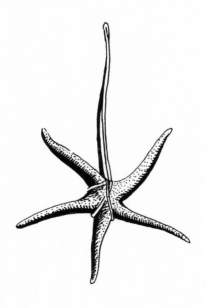

CHAPTER XI

Aghvook is Coming

TOOZAK followed his father out through the entrance-way. Apangalook stopped to look all about, to feel the air. They crossed over to the meat rack; Toozak felt the snow under his feet soft and heavy. Winter had suddenly weakened. No fog, warm sun, a softness in the wind, patches of bare ground and refuse heaps showing up.

At the meat rack, Toozak gave his father a hand, and Apangalook swung up on the upright whale jaw forming one corner of the meat rack, got a foot up onto the wooden platform, and rolled over the edge. Toozak looked back toward the other houses. "Yes, here they come; they soon know if there is anything going on." Children and dogs! They came running and formed a circle under the rack.

Then there was Wohtillin, hurrying, and Timkaroo and Tatoowi and all the rest of Apangalook's boat crew. They came and stood silent and important beside the rack. Tomorrow was the new moon of April. Today they must prepare for Apangalook's whaling worship.

The rest of the villagers who were not of Apangalook's family passed back and forth about their business, politely pretending not to notice that anything went on. Their whale worships had already been held, some in November, some in February and March. Apangalook's people had always held theirs in April, the Moon of Bird Slings.

Apangalook on the rack and the others on the ground now pulled on new sealskin mitts. "Whoosh," Toozak and Tatoowi flung gravel at the dogs. They could not risk having the sacrificial food touched or sniffed at. Very cautiously, Apangalook lifted a certain walrus hide covering in the center of the rack and drew from beneath it, first, a bundle of dried codfish. This he lowered very slowly into Wohtillin's waiting hands. Next came a bag made from the bladder of a deer, carefully tied. It held deer fat purchased from the people across in the old land and treasured for this important day of ceremony. Timkaroo received the precious thing. Toozak stood very still, wondering what would be his share to carry, for this was his first ceremony as part of his father's crew.

Finally, Apangalook handed down a seal poke to him, and smiled at his youngest hunter. "All was safe under the skin this time. Now we must get it safely into the house."

Yes, fortunate again. The sacrificial food had not been touched or tasted by anyone. A person doomed to misfortune, is he who by mistake might eat the sacrificial food. Apangalook and his crew marched into the house, Toozak last, stepping very carefully, the seal poke in his arms. All winter long he had been doing new things, and here was one thing more important than all others.

No one from any other family would be allowed inside Apangalook's house this day, and no one would come out of it until the mild day had ended and dusk and quiet had slid over the island.

. . . . .

Night came, and in Apangalook's house all but Apangalook slept. At least, all but he were supposed to be asleep; but Toozak lay awake. Toozak that curious, wide-eyed one. He saw his father sit down alone by the center post, on the floor. Before him were the dishes of the sacrifice, used only at this time. The smallest wooden dish held the reindeer fat which Assoonga had chopped up fine and made into a paste by adding walrus oil and snow. She was arrayed in her ceremonial clothes, white shirt made of walrus intestine leather, trimmed with tufts of baby seal hair. She had molded the paste into an oval cake, and she had made a little hollow in the top of the cake in which lay another small ball of the fat.

The medium-sized wooden dish held the sour greens, also molded into an oval shape with a hollow on top in which were small balls of greens. All these things Toozak had seen done. In the large platter he had seen the men place the codfish, cut into pieces the size of a fist. During all this work they had all, of course, worn mitts, so that no human flesh would touch the food.

Now Apangalook sat alone and surveyed it all. Carefully he covered the dishes with a flat sealskin. He looked up at the ceiling, from which hung two sealskin whaling pokes, inflated and ready as for the hunting. One hung at the north end of the house, the other at the south. He looked at his fine old steering paddle, and his stone-tipped lance, both lashed to the center post, and lastly he gazed at his charm bag. His it was now. It had been his father's and his grandfather's. Someday it would be Timkaroo's. Precious and helpful it was, above all things a man could own. Power had grown with it through all the long years, and that power must be guarded. No person outside the family must be allowed to touch or see its contents.

An ordinary hunting bag it might seem to be, but Apangalook knew what powerful charms it held. As he sat and gazed at it he saw in his mind the dried eyeballs of all the whales caught in his family, dried parts of the sex organs of those whales, two small rocks which had the natural shape of whales, and two pieces of sacred black rock which could be seen through. Apangalook's grandfather had said this kind of rock fell from the skies, therefore was sacred, but, above all these things, the eyes of the whale were the most powerful. Toozak, lying there so still, so watchful, knew what his father must be thinking. Only today, he, Toozak, had been shown the contents of the charm bag. He could lie here and think about it, too.

Apangalook crossed his legs, threw back his head, closed his eyes. The great time of all the moons had come. And here he was, strong and calm, ready. Only one thing more. Apangalook opened his mouth now, and with all his heart, with prayers in his soul, sang. He sang his own hunting songs, secret songs never breathed outside his house. And with those songs pouring over his ears, Toozak finally slept.

But Apangalook, the captain, kept on. All through the dark hours he sang to the greatest spirit of all, the spirit who sends Aghvook the whale to sustain Inuit.

The joy of pursuit, the joy of success, the keeping of his name as chief whale captain in the village, to say nothing of the delicious food, the baleen, the bones, could the great spirit deny him these?

Apangalook did his part—he sang on and on. These were his hours of communion with the spirits, and as he sang he felt his soul travel out of him to find and entreat the great Keyaghunuk, Spirit of the Whale.

Apangalook was still sitting there when Assoonga woke and began silently to dress again in her ceremonial clothing. No words were spoken. The others woke and quickly dressed. Wohtillin, Tatoowi, and Timkaroo arrived. Silently they took down their harpoons and went out of the house. Apangalook took his charm bag and his paddle and led the way.

Soon Pungwi, Apangalook's Striker, arrived. The boat had been lifted off the rack and was ready for the ceremony. All the paddles were in place and the charm bag hung in the bow. The boat had not been used in hunting for ten days, so that it would be clean and suitable. Assoonga now took from her clothing bag a piece of long white reindeer hair and fastened it behind her right ear. She picked up the dish of sour greens and walked slowly from the house. The men picked up the other two dishes and followed her.

Slowly Assoonga walked to the shore, to the boat rack. She passed under the rack, the others following at quite a distance, and over to the boat which lay on the ground, pointing west. Assoonga went on around the captain's steering paddle, which also lay on the ground, pointing west. Clear round the boat they walked, very slowly now, the rest of the crew standing silently at each side.

Toozak, standing in place at a ceremony for the first time, was almost afraid his breathing would make too loud a sound. He watched his mother stop close to the center of the boat and place her offering in the bottom. Pungwi and Kulukhon did likewise. Assoonga's part was over now. She retraced a solemn way back to the house, going under the boat rack as before. At no other time, Toozak knew, could anyone walk under a boat rack.

Apangalook and his crew now stepped up to the boat; they had already placed under it, bow and stern, the two short boat sleds with split tusk runners, and now they pushed the boat down over the soft snow to the water's edge where the shore ice had already begun to float off, and where the tumbled hummocks of ice were beginning to melt and send little rivers down the beach.

Even now, Toozak's curious eyes had to rove about, and suddenly they caught a glimpse of a movement up the shore. Toozak knew that figure—he had spied it at other times, in half dark, under meat racks, behind the houses! For one instant that clear sharp profile stood out against the misty light of the eastern sky, and Toozak saw the lips moving, then the figure was gone, behind Ozook's house, but Toozak knew. Walanga, offering prayers to the evil spirits, to ruin all Apangalook's ceremony, to bring him bad fortune instead of good! This was to be his revenge on the young boy who had been too smart for him at Kukulik!

All in a flash, in one turn of his head, one glance of his quick eyes, Toozak saw and knew. Icy fear like a knife thrust went through him from head to toe and sickened him. Quickly he looked at his father, at the rest of the crew. None had seen. All he could do was pray harder than he ever had, and hope that his prayers might be stronger than Walanga's. This was what came to smart boys who snared unwelcome lovers in dark passageways! He faced the east again, making no sign, only his lips moving silently. Here they all stood, watching that eastern sky, waiting.

The sea with its burden of scattered floes was very quiet this morning. There was, strangely, no wind, and the sun, when at last it pushed a red rim into the soft gray sky, seemed to do so very gently and quietly.

Now was the time. Apangalook lifted the small ball of fat from the dish in the boat and breaking it into tiny pieces, tossed them into the water, into the air, chanting his secret formulas for good luck in hunting, and toward the mountain, calling the names of his ancestors buried there, they who had passed on to him these secret formulas and songs, the charm bag, all the knowledge of how things must be done.

Apangalook did the same with the sour greens and the codfish, always breaking them into such tiny pieces that no dog could find and eat them, for that would displease Keyaghunuk. Now he and Wohtillin passed the dishes about among the others. Each silent man took what food he could hold with three fingers, and tossed it into his mouth.

When the other villagers came out of their houses, the sun was bright, and Apangalook and his crew were lashing the boat back up on its rack with lashings of walrus rope. Apangalook's ceremony was finished. He and Pungwi walked slowly up from the boat rack, too full of thought to speak easily. Would Keyaghunuk, the great one, accept their offerings? When they had reached the house, Apangalook spoke. "You, my Striker, will of course remember that neither you nor I must eat food of other people until whaling season is over? We do not want the whale which may be for us delivered into the harpoons of others whose food we have eaten."

"All the necessary things I will remember," answered Pungwi, "and I think the days of Aghvook's coming are not far off; the ice is breaking fast and the month of sailing comes quickly."

The time of Aghvook's coming! Toozak, bearing the last of the dishes of the sacrifice, stopped behind Pungwi, and that cold knife of horror twisted through him again. Could he pray strongly enough?

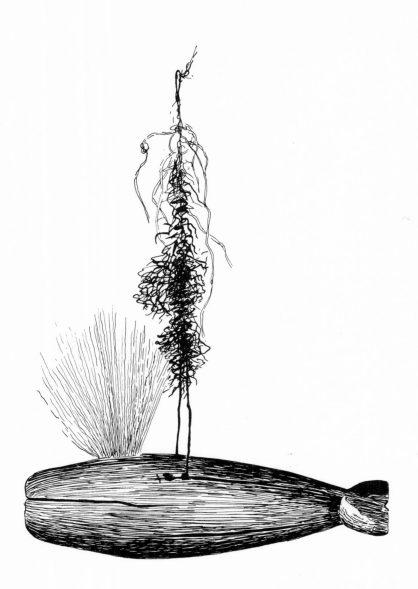

·KEGUMAHNA·
Summer-Woman Moon

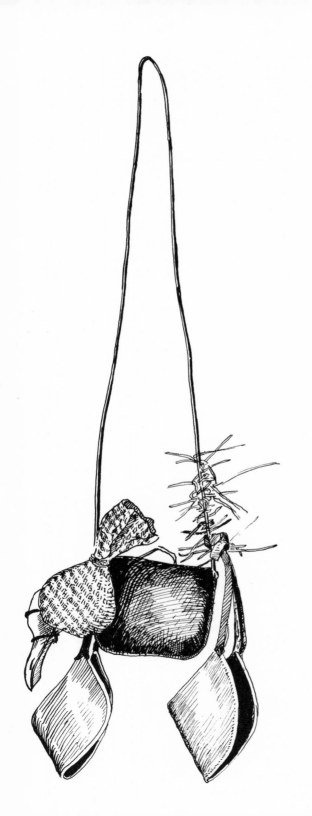

CHAPTER XII

Aghvook Comes

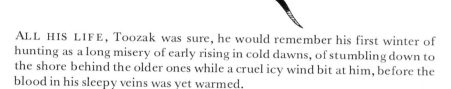

ALL HIS LIFE, Toozak was sure, he would remember his first winter of hunting as a long misery of early rising in cold dawns, of stumbling down to the shore behind the older ones while a cruel icy wind bit at him, before the blood in his sleepy veins was yet warmed.

Now it was spring and dawn came earlier, but the hunters made up for that by rising in the middle of the night, so as to be out hunting with the first light; the wind was still cruel. Toozak wondered if he were the only one who noticed these things. Of course he kept it to himself; a hunter only thinks of the urgent doings of the chase, and all one heard now in the village was Aghvook and Iviek, whale and walrus. Of all the moons, this one was the most important.

Apangalook, with calm, strong steps, walked up and down before his boat through the dark hours of each night to guard it from visits of rivals who might pray to the evil spirits to give him bad luck in the hunt; then he roused his crew before daylight and set out for the long hours in the boat. Day after day this went on, and there were no whales. And all the while Toozak lived with that awful knowing that there was one soul praying to bring them bad luck! Yet he dared not tell Apangalook. He could only keep on offering his own young prayers. Certainly this was something to make one grow out of childhood quickly. Toozak felt old these days.

· · · · ·

The edges of the ice floes were bluer than the blue flowers which bloom on the sandspit in July, as blue as the flowers and as green as their leaves. A laughing little breeze made deep blue ripples in front of the boat; the sky was that same blue, and mountains of white clouds like giants' ningloos

95

were sailing about up there. A male sawbill duck[1] flew right in front of Toozak's face. He waved his paddle but missed him, and the other boys laughed. The duck was chasing a female, round and round, climbing into the air, streaking downward.

As the crew sailed and paddled steadily out toward more open water, they heard geese passing high overhead. Now a flock of puffins came swishing by, close to the water, and behind them, a cloud of Least Auklets![2] Whee-ee—the auklets again! Every man in the boat shouted and laughed, nodded to his neighbor, waved greetings to the auklets. Spring was really come, then—the auklets were back, and hunters could carry boiled meat in the whaling boats. Not until the auklets came was this permitted.

Hi-hi, winter was gone! Birds, clouds, sunshine, blue ripples and blue floats of ice all proclaimed it. A little flock of plovers flew over the boat. Toozak wondered how it felt to be one of those swift-flying ones. They made his heart lighter somehow. He stroked along easily. The very boat seemed lighter since the sun had come out and they had seen the birds. If only they could see—"Ah-eee," Toozak dropped his paddle, jumped to his feet, started to point, snatched his hand back as though he had burned it, then, clasping both hands behind his back, nodded his head to the left and said in a small trembling voice, "There is Aghvook."

Instantly, they were all paddling like demons! Toozak paddled too, but still trembling. Kulukhon brought the walrus-stomach sail about and sat with eager face, holding the line and watching Apangalook for orders.

Poor Toozak! He breathed a great sigh. What a narrow escape! He had had the good fortune to see the first whale, and then had nearly insulted him by pointing a finger at him. Aghvook and the all-powerful Keyaghunuk who sent him were so easily offended, every consideration must be shown them. Toozak's heart pounded in his throat. He paddled fiercely, not even glancing at Tatoowi who paddled beside him. One of the great moments of life had just come and his thoughts were whirling like a flock of kittiwakes. Only this he realized: they must paddle and watch Apangalook for orders, and perhaps Keyaghunuk would listen to their prayers rather than to those of that handsome evil one back in the village.

They were fairly flying over the smooth dark sea, and there was the tall plume of Aghvook's breath, much closer than the first time. He was traveling almost toward them, heading north along the island coast. Every man was tense, putting every ounce of strength into his strokes. Aghvook disappeared. "Slower now," spoke Apangalook softly, "see where he comes up next."

Kulukhon took in the sail. Quietly they slid along; even their breathing seemed too loud. "Whoosh,"—only fifty yards away, a fountain of hot steam rose into the air, and up came a great black back which gleamed a moment in the sun. The crew held the boat motionless and waited for the black hulk to sink again.

Apangalook's eyes were like the stars of a cold winter sky; his thick lips were pressed into a flat line; the veins in his temples throbbed. He looked at Pungwi in the bow, and Pungwi looked back at him and nodded. "This time we try," said Apangalook softly, and the boat shot forward again. Pungwi rose in the bow, planted his feet solidly, examined once more the ivory head of his harpoon, the lines leading from it. From the tail of his eye, he could see that Timkaroo and Tatoowi were poised to drop their paddles and throw over the three pokes.

They paddled on in the course Aghvook had taken. Toozak had by now gotten the signal poke, a special inflated sealskin, fastened to a slender pole which he held up as high as he could and waved, and then lashed in the stern behind his father's seat. He glanced back over the water and ice and saw that two boats back there already had their pokes up; they had seen the signal and would be coming.

Toozak had no time to look further. Aghvook was almost under them. Up came his wet breath again. "Oh, hoh," spoke Apangalook sharply. Swiftly he swerved the boat to the left of the whale and yet more swiftly they paddled. Pungwi lifted his long harpoon over his head; right up almost onto the whale's shoulder the boat sped, then Aghvook's back began sliding up out of the water, and Pungwi struck. He meant that harpoon to go clear through Aghvook's eight inches of blubber and stay there, and that is what it did. At the same instant Timkaroo and Tatoowi, both sitting on the right side, threw over the pokes of Pungwi's harpoon.

Aghvook went down like a rock, flicking his enormous flukes as he went and enveloping his hunters with a great salt wave. But they could not notice that. Timkaroo was watching the coil of rope as it payed out. To get caught in that meant sure death. Tons of mighty flesh were pulling that line down, deep under. The rest of the crew were paddling furiously to get clear. Under the water went the pokes. Pungwi's harpoon was holding so far!

Apangalook now raised his paddle straight up into the air and shouted out with a great voice, "Wo-ho-ho, ho-ho."

Again he raised his paddle high and "Wo-ho-ho, ho-ho" rang out, again.

Apangalook's boat had struck a whale. Toozak began to feel younger!

Now the chase began.

Two pokes and a long black back were up again and through the water they raced. Aghvook was towing them along at a furious speed. Apangalook's face was set, but gleaming with excitement as he steered to keep them free of the line. White spume flew from the boat's bow; the breeze of their passage whistled in their ears. Toozak felt he was being carried along in a mad dream, a sorcerer's dream; things had become too exciting to be real. They all sat quiveringly alert, paddles poised, streams of sweat pouring down over their faces. After all the thought and planning, the songs and sacrifices, here they were, actually in the midst of a battle with Aghvook, the greatest beast.

Pungwi lifted his great stone-tipped spear, but they all knew they could not hope to spear Aghvook yet; they had to have help, more harpoons, more pokes.

Toozak hardly dared look around, but he sensed boats coming up behind them. First came Wohtillin's, its crew swaying in unbelievable speed, taking in their sail and approaching from the other side of the whale, Ozook poised in the bow. Ozook, father of that Walanga, ignorant of his son's doings, about to help kill Apangalook's whale! Aghvook perhaps realized now that he was pulling more than his own weight. He slowed a bit, and in that moment Wohtillin's boat sped up close and Ozook struck.

Ozook was one of the best, and they needed the best this day. Two true strikes. Down went Aghvook, and this time Wohtillin's crew was backing frantically away from the tumult of his descent. For he was angry now. Something was bothering him too much. The great hulk rolled and shook as it went down and raised the sea into real waves.

Both boats pulled their lines straight and the men breathed a moment, for now Aghvook had six pokes fastened to him and it would be harder and harder to stay down. Come up he must, and here were the rest of the boats now, four of them, Irrigoo's first, holding off to the side, ready to come in and strike.

So it went. Hours of racing headlong behind the angry giant, far out westward, till the island began to lose its height; back again, straight for shore, and toward floating ice cakes, where everyone was breathless, and Apangalook's were not the only lips which moved in silent pleading with the great Spirit. If the whale dove under one of those, the line must be cut, and the quarry, with lines, pokes, and harpoons would all be lost.

And crueler yet, all knew that the loss, thus, of a whale once struck would mean loss also of a member of the captain's family. So it had always been. This fear was forever with them and froze their hearts into a cold misery whenever Aghvook headed toward ice. Even in the loose slush ice there was plenty of danger from fouled lines, and every paddle was busy. Toozak shivered and at the same time felt sweat running down his cheeks. It seemed that he was living years of his life flying along over that blue water.

Aghvook had three boats on him now and still it went on; the breeze increased a little; the white clouds scudded faster in the blue sky; the sea was darker. Kittiwakes cried overhead, the puffins, murres and auklets skimmed back and forth, and fulmars, the whale birds,[3] had also sensed the thing which would interest them and glided and wheeled about on quiet wings, watching that queer scene. A long blackness streaking through the water with upright seals wavering along on top of it, and racing along behind, three boats with six stiff figures in each one—so it looked to the fulmars' eyes. It also looked like a big meal for fulmars before long!

Toozak was really surprised when he came out of the trance of excitement and realized it was still daylight when Aghvook was finally tired and the lances of Pungwi and Ozook could find his heart. They were fortunate. They had been able to lance the whale on one of his trips toward shore, so that towing in was not the back-breaking long ordeal it sometimes was. They had seen many other whales blowing during that day but the boats had stayed with Apangalook. They knew his whale was a big one and it would take all their forces to get him in.

Now Apangalook stepped to the bow and from the outside of his charm bag took two beaked eye-shields of young mukluk skin, fastened one on his own forehead, handed the other to Pungwi. This was a day of triumph for these two; it was only right that the people should be able to see who had struck the whale.

Aghvook floated there, harmless, wonderful great hulk, great gift to Inuit. The boats floated about at a little distance. What a good feeling, now, for all the crews, to drop paddles and slump in their seats and rest a bit while Apangalook did the next thing. Toozak and Tatoowi found time to look at each other now, and smile, and Toozak felt all the worries and all the old age flying away. He felt good inside for the first time in weeks, and he would be so glad to smile into Walanga's face when they brought Aghvook in!

The boat was paddled slowly to Aghvook's side, just in front of his tail, and started slowly around, close to the black body. Apangalook raised his paddle and shouted, "Wo-ho-ho;" slowly they paddled along to Aghvook's head. "Wo-ho-ho." Around they slid to the other side of his head. "Wo-ho-ho." Along the side, close to the flukes again, once more Apangalook's voice rang out over the water, "Wo-ho-ho!"

Now to work. Some cutting up must be done before they towed him in. Keen-edged stone blades, fastened to long handles, now came into every man's hand, and all the boats clustered about, against that quiet body. All life, all fierceness was gone from it; it had become merely a mass of food, of building material, of fuel, for the small lively creatures clustered about it.

Everyone was cutting. Of course Apangalook and his crew would have half the slabs, and all flukes and flippers, eye and nostrils. Apangalook himself leaned over and carefully removed the eyes, the nostrils. The center part of the fluke was cut out and leaned carefully in the very bow of the boat. Behind this, Apangalook and Pungwi carefully laid the eyes, in the bottom of the boat, behind these, the nostrils, then the flippers, and finally, a little astern of the middle of the boat, the ends of the flukes. In Apangalook's boat, things were always done in exactly the proper manner.

Now they were ready to fill the boat with slabs, with long sections of baleen, and finally to tow the rest of the monster in, the pokes still attached and helping to hold him up. And Apangalook did not forget to present two slabs of skin and blubber each to the old men who were in the other boats. It would be dangerous to be forgetful of the old.

They were perhaps a mile and half from shore, and everyone bent to his stroke with a will, and the sails went up again. They were all tasting in anticipation the excitement in the village, the joy of women and children, the delicious flavor of success in hunting—also the delicious flavor of munktuk. Feasting and song and unrestrained mirth there would be on Sevuokuk this night.

The fifth and last boat to arrive at the scene of the chase took its place next to the whale's head and fastened its line firmly into the body. The fourth boat came next, then the third, then Irrigoo's boat, then Wohtillin's, and leading the whole line, Apangalook's.

Approaching the land, Apangalook and his crew raised their paddles and shouted the call of triumph, "Wo-ho-ho, ho-ho," and again, when they were very close in and could see all the eager crowd on shore, loudly, happily, they sang out, "Wo-ho-ho—ho-ho."

None shouted more loudly than Toozak.

CHAPTER XIII

Baleen and Munktuk

THE GENTLE SURF lifted the triumphant boat upon the beach and Apangalook and Pungwi, still wearing their beaks, leaped out. The crowd on the beach, bursting with excitement but politely silent, stood back, and Apangalook, carrying his paddle, and Pungwi, carrying his lance, strode up the sloping shore and disappeared in Apangalook's house. They knew Assoonga would have heard the news and be waiting, but of course she must not put on her ceremonial clothes until the men came for her.

The two most important men in Sevuokuk village that day stood, silent but exuding great joy, while the woman hurried into the beautiful white parka, the new boots, and tied the white reindeer hair to her right braid.

When Assoonga was ready, she took from the corner a small wooden pail, filled it with water from the big dish under the platform, and into the water dropped small pieces of nunivak.

Now Apangalook led the way back to the boat. Assoonga followed behind the two men, stepping carefully, her sweet face very solemn. They stepped back into the boat, while she stood on the shore in front of it. Each one of the crew took his place and lifted his paddle as though to stroke. With Pungwi standing in the bow, they rocked the boat back and forth, and Assoonga swayed back and forth with them, rocking her body as the boat rocked. The clustered boats, out beyond and around the whale, the people on the shore, were quiet, watching this last ceremony.

Apangalook lifted his paddle, pointing the tip toward the south, and Assoonga held up her pail, reaching to the south. Apangalook once more shouted the whale cry, "Wo-ho-ho," several times, shifted his paddle to the other side and repeated that loud glad cry.

Assoonga stepped down close to the boat and with trembling hands passed her pail to Pungwi. What woman would not tremble? She was the most honored woman in the village this day, and she knew all the other women were watching each thing she did, watching and remembering.

Pungwi passed the pail to the captain, who took a mouthful of water and one piece of nunivak and passed it to Kulukhon. Each man drank and ate; they were great men of the village today. Toozak had never had quite such a feeling as this was. The pail came round to Pungwi; again he drank and passed it over to Assoonga. She stood very still now, holding the pail with both hands, eyes on Pungwi's face.

Pungwi slowly lifted his harpoon, took aim, struck. The shaft clattered into the gravel between Assoonga's legs—a true strike, just as he had made in the hunt that morning. The ceremony was over.

Now were the bonds untied! Now were the tongues unleashed! The birds had followed the procession in and were flying about and crying in many tones, but they could not equal the people themselves. No sleep that night for anyone. The sun sank out of sight, but darkness did not come, and through the mild half-light of May, amid a babble of voices, snatches of song, much laughter, screaming of birds, Aghvook was cut up.

All the slabs off first, but not cutting quite all the blubber off, for some must be left on to keep the whale afloat until they were quite through with him. Walrus hide lines must be pulled under him in several places and fastened to boats on each side. Frequently Apangalook ordered the lines tightened, and Aghvook's hulk would lift a little higher, so they could keep on cutting. Apangalook worked as hard as any, but he also watched everything and gave orders; his word was law this night.

Fulmars came and perched on the whale and picked busily away at the blubber. Toozak laughingly poked one aside with his long knife. "Go on, you can eat, but try to keep out of the way of the knife if you can; every minute you are getting clumsier; soon the fat will be running from your eyes and you won't be able to get off the water."

Toozak slit a narrow bit of munktuk from the slab he was working on and popped it into his mouth. Nothing could be more delicious; if all the good things in life could be rolled into one and tasted, he thought it would taste like munktuk. He laughed aloud again. Relief, excitement, pride—they were all pushing the merry laughter through his lips.

The pile of slabs on the shore was mounting. Soon they could perhaps, with the whole village helping, haul the great carcass up the steeply sloping shore above the water and have it safe. Meanwhile the joyous work went on and on through the half-dark.

When the sun came again, Apangalook trudged up to his house with all the crews. Much had happened since the last dawn, and they were tired. There, before the house, was a high heap of slabs. They all stood looking at this small mountain of food. Every soul in the village had helped to drag these up, and everyone would have munktuk and meat and oil. But it had been too much for Sekwo and Notangi! There behind the pile of slabs the two little people lay, curled up, sound asleep.

Toozak leaned on the handle of his long whale knife. All his bones felt as soft as the strips of baleen lying there. He saw Assoonga come out of the house bearing a flaming lamp. She set it down among the pieces of the flukes, and beside it, placed a wooden platter of nunivak.

Apangalook stepped to the fire, picked up bits of nunivak and tossed them into the air, naming the names of all the great spirits, especially Keyaghunuk, to whom they were offering thanks. To the men of all the crews he then passed the platter. There remained still a thing or two to do before anyone could rest. The young men gathered up the points of the flukes, the middle section, and the flippers, and carried them to the house. The other parts of the flukes which had been especially laid aside they carried to the meat cellar and there laid them in the same position as they had in the boat, the pieces of flukes on the northwest side of the cellar. The next thing was to divide the slabs among the crews, each man lugging away his share to his own meat cellar.

And lastly, the middle section and points of the flukes must be tied with a thong and pulled up to the top of the center post of Apangalook's house, with the charm bag hung below them. Toozak wondered why, when he had been a boy and only watching these things, he had not noticed how much work there was to bringing a whale in. "Come you now, Toozak," he heard his father calling. "Bring the three pokes. Fasten them on top of the roof of this house, the sign that we have killed a whale."

Apangalook was bringing his paddle to the front of the house. Here he stuck it in the ground, its point leaning toward the west. Pungwi, weary but glad, set his lance at the right side of the door, point up. Apangalook looked at him. "This was a good day, Striker."

Pungwi merely nodded, but Toozak saw the blood rise in his cheeks. Pungwi understood that the captain was well pleased with his Striker's performance. Everything had gone well. Toozak had been looking for Walanga, but he was not to be seen this night, it seemed. Toozak had wanted the pleasure of looking into that handsome face and smiling!

Pungwi lifted a big bundle of baleen, his share of the precious bone, to his shoulder, and smiled at Apangalook. "I think it will not be hard for you and me to stay inside these five days. Much sleep and rest will be welcome."

Apangalook and Assoonga stood alone at last. The meat was on the racks, the munktuk in the cellar, the baleen on the rack. To be sure, their whale was not all gone yet, but it could wait. It was morning, misty and cool, but a warm color filtered through the clouds on the eastern sky behind the mountain. The village still buzzed. Down on the shore, the last one of the boats was being hauled up. Aghvook lay there, and the young people were racing and laughing along the beach.

Ever since Ozook's crew had brought in the first baby walrus the week before, the young ones had been free to play ball, and Apangalook and Assoonga both smiled when they saw Toozak and Tatoowi, who had moaned with weariness when they dragged the last slab of munktuk to the cellar, now jumping high in the air to snatch the grass-filled ball of sealskin, crying "Tukka, tukka," in voices as strong as any!

Swift as a white fox and more graceful than any bird, Apangalook saw Yahoh's young Okoma flying around the edge of the crowd, his slim Toozak leaping at her side. Okoma, eh? Perhaps it would have to be Okoma. It was easy to see that she was swiftest and strongest of all the girls.

Yes, it was so, in the magic moon of spring hunting, the "Summer Woman" moon. Apangalook sighed deeply and turned to his well-earned rest with a happy heart. With the gift of Aghvook the spirits had shown their good will toward Inuit. Fears could be laid away for a while. A blessing had enveloped the whole village, the breeze, the returning sun, the voices of the birds, the great stretches of ice-free ocean, all spoke this blessing from above.

Now Apangalook and Pungwi must stay in for five days, while the other boats went out. And while they stayed in, they must paint the paddle, the paint would be made from lamp soot and the liquid from the eyeballs of the whale, and the image would be that of Aghvook. Apangalook's weary body sank into rest, while the gay voices of youth still came through the morning, while his young son forgot weariness and knew only exultation.

Toozak had never known such a day—such a night. And now the morning again, soft and mild, made for youth and hot spirits, and always, that swift laughing-eyed Okoma, there, yet leaping away from him, just beyond his reach.

· PENAHVEK ·
Moon When Rivers Begin to Flow

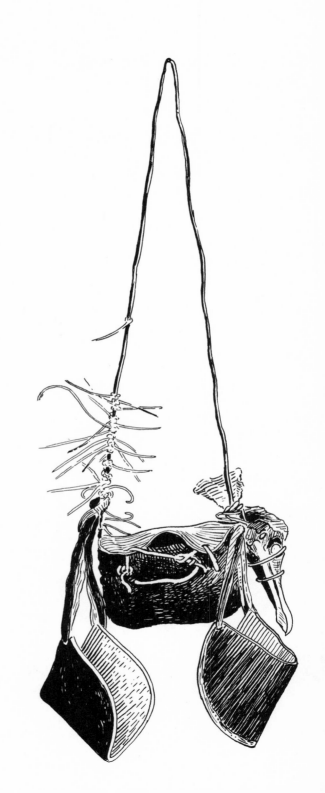

CHAPTER XIV

The Sorcerer Dreams

MASSIU walked slowly through the village. The snow was gone, the ground drying. The air was mild and full of the cries of birds. In and out they flew; up above the mountain they circled and dipped. Down in the rocks, auklets chattered and twittered; on the cliff ledges, murres gabbled and clacked; puffins hurried about, beating their wings frantically; cormorants stretched out their long necks and streaked away, out over the blue water, beyond the whaling fleet. The black cliffs of the Cape Mountain had become alive again.

From the lake at the base of the mountain, Massiu heard the whistling of plovers, the soft, cooing, "Ah-ow, ah-ow" of eiders, and in the air above his head the bright-feathered longspur[1] dipped and swirled and poured out his rippling song. Massiu did not feel that any horror could happen in such a place, yet he must go to the elders of the village.

Apangalook was not out whaling today. He and Wohtillin and Ikmallowa and several of the old men sat on the great council rocks at the center of the village; outside the circle of rocks, Toozak and Tatoowi ran slowly round and round, doing their daily exercise. Ikmallowa was leaning forward, hands moving, telling a story. But he saw Massiu coming. He looked at him keenly, and stopped the storytelling. "You have something to say to us, Massiu?"

Massiu looked at Apangalook. It was suddenly very quiet. The two boys dropped down on the ground behind Ikmallowa—there was only the crying of birds above the cliff and the roar of surf below, on the beach. Massiu sat down on one of the big stones, facing the group of older men. "Think of it what you will, men of Sevuokuk, but I have had a dream, and I saw strangers upon Sevuokuk. I saw knives flying through the air, red with

107

blood. It may be that some spirit sends me these dreams as warning. The hunters must be careful in their whaling ceremonies; it may be that something has been done carelessly and that trouble may come of it."

Apangalook looked at his father. "What say you, Ikmallowa?"

Ikmallowa spoke very quietly and they listened in deep silence. Toozak felt the blood pounding in his ears, he was listening so hard. "You know I have told you how my grandfather made armor, and of the bad Inuit from across the water who came in the old days."

Ikmallowa paused. "I remember that armor. I think we shall make some more. I think all the old men will make more new arrows with sharp stone heads. The women will make quivers of sealskin for them. The young men will exercise more each day than they have done in the past. We will be ready."

No one spoke. Toozak wondered what other new thing was to happen in these first hunting years of his. He and Tatoowi looked at Apangalook with wide eyes, and Apangalook knew what was in all the minds—enemies coming, when they remembered none but peaceable folk coming over the water? Massiu was young. He had not been a Singer long. Could he know? And yet, the ice was nearly all gone; people could be coming over any time. Apangalook knew they would do as Ikmallowa said.

So evening came, and the four boats which had been out hunting came back and found strange things going on in the long daylight of spring.

In the center of the village they found Apangalook, Ikmallowa and Wohtillin squatted around a dried walrus hide, busy with stone knives. Beside the walrus hide was also the newly-stretched skin of a mukluk Timkaroo had brought in a few days before.

Strips of walrus, double thickness, alternated with strips of mukluk, double thickness, then a wooden breastplate and wooden strips covered with mukluk, from shoulder to wrist along the back of the arm. Ikmallowa was fastening all the strips into place with thongs. Gradually the mighty arrow-defeating shirt was taking shape. Pungwi gazed in silence; he had heard stories of such armor but had never thought to live to see such things being done on Sevuokuk in his day. A man goes out whaling in the morning and comes home to find the whole village in queer doings. He watched Wohtillin holding a big piece of walrus hide flat while his clever Rohltungu cut a great square shield from it with her oolak. So, even the women were in this affair! "And what, Ikmallowa, is that?" he asked at last, pointing to Rohltungu's work.

"That," answered Ikmallowa, "will be fastened and stand up behind the warrior's shoulder. No arrows from behind can harm him. All the rest of the armor will hang from these strong mukluk straps over the shoulders."

Pungwi looked about. Behind the armor makers sat all the old men, stern of face, making arrows. Toozak, Tatoowi, Kulukhon and all the rest of the young men were exercising. They were going about the circle, lifting the stones, one after another. But some they could not budge. Some of those stones had never been lifted by anyone; they lay there, a challenge to every man. Wohtillin had lifted all but the three big ones on the south side. Timkaroo stooped and strained at one of these. The others laughed.

"That's right; keep on, Timkaroo! Someday maybe you will be another Wohtillin."

At last Pungwi had to ask a question. "What goes on in this village, since morning?"

Apangalook answered, "Massiu has had a dream, a warning. We are going to be ready for strangers coming from afar, but I think it makes only a fine game, for the young ones." He smiled at the antics of all those boys who were trying to become strong all at once.

Pungwi looked out beyond the village toward the mountain and saw three figures running toward the village. They had been "running the circle," out behind the village, around the lake, back along the base of the mountain, to the village again, three miles. Every day in summer they ran this before eating. It was the regular exercise for young hunters. Yet now there was something different in the way they were going about it. The first runner came loping up to Pungwi; this was Kaka, his own son, barely fourteen, but the fleetest runner in the village. Pungwi laughed. "Well done, Kaka. Those eel charms you wear must be more powerful than any others."

Kaka looked down at the two little dried eels flapping on the leg band of his boots; speed and endurance they gave him. If running could defeat enemies, Kaka would defend Sevuokuk with honor.

Pungwi ran beside him and they came to the circle of stones and the busy people again. Toozak and all the others were jumping now, and Kaka joined them. Around the circle they ran, jumping over each stone in the way. The old men looked up from their arrow-making and remembered how swiftly they had once made that round, leaping and yelling. And now cold and damp and frost and bitter days on the ice and the seasons rolling over had brought them to arrow-making, and watching and smiling at the strength and speed of grandsons. Ikmallowa forgot this serious business of arrow-making long enough to cry, "Hi, hi," when Toozak came flying over the largest stone.

Later in the evening there was the ball game on the beach, as always. It was a calm, mild evening. Danger, warfare, trouble—they were words only. They meant nothing to these young people. For despite fears and warnings and armor-making, this was still the glad Summer-Woman month, the moon when hugs and kisses and love-making on the beach were the custom, enjoyed by all, young and old.

"Tukka, tukka," arms outstretched, each one calls for the ball. What screaming and laughter! Up in the air it goes. Toozak snatches it, but three other players are on top of him and they all go down in the sand in a heap of furry legs and arms. Toozak finds himself holding Okoma in a firm embrace, at last, and presses his nose to hers in a fervent kiss; then off they race after the screaming crowd, again, "Tukka, tukka, tukka, hey, hey."

The surf whispered lovingly to the shore. The sun melted away behind a bank of mist and the sky began to darken a little, yet still the sounds of springtime went on. "Tukka, tukka, hey, hey." Toozak and Okoma flying faster than all the others. They could hardly find the ball in the dusk, but they found each other. Ah, it was even pleasanter than he had imagined!

CHAPTER XV

Toozak Runs

TOOZAK was running in a different direction this morning. Instead of running the circle, he was running straight down the coast toward the southwest.

Days had passed; armor had been made, another whale had been brought in, by Wohtillin this time. The ball games, the love-making, the misty mild weather—all life went on quite as usual, and fears of strange enemies were fading. Keyaghunuk had sent them another whale; surely everything must be all right.

Toozak was not worrying. He ran and never tired and felt strong and safe. Beyond the fox trap lines, past the big lagoon, following the rugged shore, around one great headland after another he ran. The surf pounded below his feet, the birds wheeled and screamed and dove above his head. Now and then Toozak sat on a rock and breathed deeply, and idly aimed small rocks at the auklets sailing about him in the mist. Then would come the urge to go on. Toozak was enjoying this; he was going to run further today than anyone had ever run. On he went in mist and light rain and fitful sunshine. And when many long stretches of rocky beach lay behind him, he climbed over a great cape, almost as high as Sevuokuk Mountain.

He was a little tired now. He lay on his stomach, on a flat, lichen-covered boulder, and pressed his hot face against the cool rock. A little breeze came sliding across the mountain top and sent delightful little cold fingers up under Toozak's light murre-skin parka. Pretty soon he was cool and breathing quietly, and he raised his head and looked below him.

There lay a perfect small cove, shaped like a new moon, dotted with rocky islets. Its beach was smooth sand and the slopes back of the beach were gentle. The vanishing snow had already left bare places which would soon be green with many kinds of small plants.

All this Toozak took in at a glance. Then his eyes widened and he flattened himself to the rock.

On an old snowdrift straight below him, a mother white bear lay, with two lively cubs climbing over her. Toozak's bewildered eyes roved over the place, widened again. On the other side of the cove, two big white fellows lay dozing. A well-worn trail led above them to the top of the slope, and on this, another bear was shouldering carelessly down toward the beach.

Toozak could not move, but his eyes could, and although it was a wonder they did not burst with the strain, they beheld two whales playing about, out in the cove. Toozak thought he must be dreaming, but he kept seeing these things. The whales dove and rolled over and thrashed at each other with their flukes. The bears looked out at the noise of the whales splashing, but returned to their naps and their playing. The big one on the beach sniffed along the tide line, lazily. Toozak saw that they must be used to whale company. And they must be used to plenty of seals to eat, for Toozak was sure the little rocky islets must be seal rocks. What a place— whales and seals and bears! What news he had now for Apangalook and the rest! He had better be starting home.

Starting home! Toozak slid onto the moss at the base of the big rock in sudden terror. Could he *get* home? Could he get away from this wonderful, awful place without being seen or smelled by Nanook? What if Nanook were a little bit hungry?

Cautiously Toozak laid his long running stick across his knees. He pulled his small hunting bag off his shoulders and felt about inside it. With a long breath he pulled out the sharp stone spear-tip his father had given him after he got that first walrus. In a few moments, Toozak had a spear, and there was no use in sitting there longer. He must get up, and start back across the top of the mountain. He only prayed that Nanook would be alone if he must meet him, Nanook of the brains like a man, Nanook who was so hard to fool.

Down over moss-covered rocks, in the bed of a tiny stream bubbling from under the snowdrifts higher up, Toozak picked a quick way and stepped softly down, eyes shifting all about him. He had left the cove behind. He dropped down onto the wet grass slope where the little stream spread out toward the beach. And Nanook came walking from behind a jumble of rocks at Toozak's side.

Toozak knew things were to happen fast. Only the talk of the old men saved him now; he remembered what to do and did it before he thought further. Nanook stopped short and raised his muzzle to sniff in interest at this new sight and new smell. In the thong about his waist, Toozak had tucked a sealskin mitt he had found in his bag. Now he stepped quickly forward and tossed the mitt into the air in front of Nanook's nose. Nanook rose on his hind legs to reach at this good seal-smelling thing, and in that instant Toozak rushed and struck.

Miles of runing and hours of jumping and of lifting stones, all were in that quick desperate thrust of spear into the white chest above him. Nanook came down. Ah, Nanook, Inuit is a little bit smarter than you! When you came down you drove that wicked point clear through your body! Flail your all-powerful arms as you will, you cannot reach your slayer and your heart is broken. What you took to be your next meal was a young hunter too smart for you.

And now Toozak did run. His running that morning through the gray mist was as nothing to the way he flew now through the bright golden evening, the running stick with the spear-point on its end stuck under his arms, behind his shoulders, so he could breathe his best. The sun sank and the sky darkened and still through the dusky hours Toozak ran. The stupendous adventure he had just been through gave power to his limbs; he could not tire. Never had he dreamed of such fame coming to a young man. He had been proud of one tattoo spot on each of his joints for his first mukluk; now he would have another for his first polar bear. They would have to come in the ungiaks and help bring his bear in. And the skull would be his to keep forever, to be placed on his grave when he died. In exultation, in monstrous relief, Toozak ran!

He came to the village just as the sun was gold behind the black rocks atop Sevuokuk Mountain and the breeze of morning was waking the sleepy birds in the cliff crannies. Toozak was not running now. He walked into the village, past Wohtillin's house. There was singing in there, and suddenly, he remembered that this was the day of the ceremonies of the end of whaling. His great news would have to wait until the worship was over.

In front of his own home, he saw Tatoowi and Timkaroo carrying the whale flukes from the cellar to the house. From inside came Apangalook's strong voice, "Ah, yunga, ah." Apangalook was singing his hunting songs again. Toozak slipped in very quietly and sat in a corner, suddenly wishing he could sleep; in his present state, nothing seemed real.

As in a dream, he saw his father sitting below the center post where hung all the hunting gear and the charm bag. Apangalook wore his whale captain's beak and held his drum. He was drumming and singing his hunting songs in a high, strong voice. Before him burned the lamp; over it hung the black wooden image of Aghvook which Toozak knew had been his father's grandfather's. On one side of the lamp lay the head of the first female walrus they had taken that season, and all around the lamp, the pieces of whale fluke.

Toozak's head nodded, and jerked upright when his father's voice suddenly ceased. The family and all the crew sat silent. Toozak watched his father as he bent over the lamp cutting walrus and whale meat into tiny pieces. The light of the lamp flickered over his intent face. "Here they are celebrating the *end* of whaling," thought Toozak half asleep. "What will they say when I tell them I saw whales *today*?"

Yet he could not violate the rule of silence during a ceremony. Apangalook put tiny pieces of meat into a wooden scoop and carried it out through the passageway. Toozak knew he was sacrificing these pieces to the air, thanking the spirits for the whales and for all favors. Massiu had warned them all to be very careful in their ceremonies. But Toozak could not stay awake; his head sank on his breast.

Sekwo nudged him; he rose, half asleep. He knew his father must have come in again and they must all get up and step on the flukes lying by the lamp. Then they could sit down again while Apangalook threw pieces of meat toward the lamp, to feed any spirits that had come to take part in the ceremony.

The next thing Toozak knew, the big platter of meat was there, and everyone was eating loudly, with greatest politeness and ceremony. Toozak tried to chew a tender piece of baby walrus, but his jaws would not work. How he longed to cry out, "Apangalook, I, your son, have killed Nanook," and tumble into sleep, but he dared not. The ceremony must never be interrupted. In the soft half-dark of the house, in the warm air heavy with odors of whale flukes and seal oil and human bodies, Toozak got sleepier and sleepier.

Now the helpful little Sekwo was pulling him to his feet. His father must have finished dividing the flukes among his family and his crew, and now they must all go around the lamp with the rest of the crew, and sing the long song of the end of whaling. Around and around, for hours it seemed, walking and singing in a waking dream. But finally the song ended, and that was the end of the ceremony.

By this time, Toozak was not sure; maybe he had *dreamed* of killing the bear, of seeing whales. As the relatives and crew began to crawl out of the house, his eye fell upon his sleeping robe, on the platform just behind him. He heard Assoonga laugh and say softly, "Our Toozak must have run all night."

He thought he heard a voice like his own say, "I, Toozak, have killed Nanook," heard his father laugh at that, and then he knew no more.

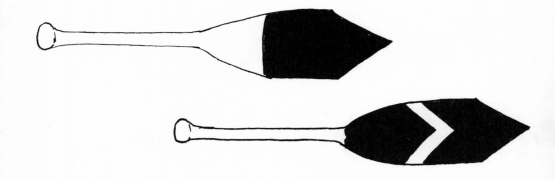

·ANGOTAHVEK·
Moon of Plant Gathering

CHAPTER XVI

On the Mountain

THE ONLY SNOW left on the island was the Aneelgulgit, that long, perpetual snowdrift along the south-west side of the inland mountains, and a few hard drifts in crannies directly under the summit of the Cape Mountain at Sevuokuk village. All else was bare gravel or gleaming vegetation. The gravel spit before the village was all blue and rose and shining white flowers. Tokoya and Ega walked among them that morning and came to the lake, to the colony of cheeping sandpipers.[1] The water was fresh and clear; the two girls knelt and drank and got their braids wet and laughed and dabbled their hands in the warm water. The sun was already high and beat down upon Sevuokuk out of a cloudless blue.

Tokoya had a sudden wild wish. She would like to pull off her feather parka and her boots and her kalevak and plunge into that clear water, but it was such a ridiculous idea she dared not even mention it to Ega, and they left the lake and walked on toward the mountain.

Jaegers[2] rose from the mossy hummocks at the mountain's base and lifted carelessly into the sky, dipping and circling above the tundra, watching the nests of sandpipers and eiders for an unguarded moment. "I would hate to be a sandpiper mother, and have to watch those thieves all the time." Tokoya stooped to gather a handful of nunivak. She carried a poke on her back, but she and Ega could take their time today. Kulukhon and Timkaroo had both gone down the shore in their small ungiak after seals. There would be no eating until late in the evening.

Up the mountain the two young wives climbed, slowly, with laughter and chatter. "I think we could not keep up with Toozak today," laughed Ega.

"Ah, that brother of mine, he thinks he is a big chief boy since he killed Nanook and discovered that good hunting place. And now I think we will

121

not see your father, Pungwi's, family very much, since they have all moved to that place Toozak found—Poowooiliak. But I am glad Toozak did not go down there with them."

Tokoya, sitting down on a mossy ledge, smiled as though some interesting memory came before her eyes. "With Toozak gone, things would seem so different in our house; it seems that where Toozak is, something interesting is happening all the time."

Ega pulled two or three round spicy leaves from out of the moss where she sat, and slipped them into her mouth. "Did you hear the story my father brought back when he came from the new village? It seems it is a fine place for whales and walrus and seals, and *too* fine for Nanook. It must have been the place the bears have lived in for a long time, for the people could find trails everywhere, and many times the bears walked right past the house and under the meat rack, and the people thought something must be done."

"What *could* they do?" Tokoya stuffed a handful of green cloudberries[3] into her mouth and sat, wide-eyed, as Ega went on.

"Oh, they did something. Pungwi went out and killed a small bear and women cut off the blubber. Then, at dusk one night, Pungwi built a fire outdoors and they started cooking bear meat. Kaka sat by the fire. Whenever the fire died down, he threw on some bear blubber to make the fire burn hard."

"What happened then?" urged Tokoya. "I never heard of such a thing being done."

Ega smiled. "The smell of the burning blubber rose into the air and Pungwi says it could be smelled all over that part of the island. The bears left, for they have not seen one since then. *I* think Nanook is pretty smart. It is not surprising that the old people say he has the brains of a person."

She laughed and rose. "Come, let us go up and look over the world."

They followed up the mossy, spongy sides of the little stream which filtered aimlessly down over the rocks from a snowdrift high up. The mountainside was a place of beauty during the brief glory of summer on Sevuokuk. The jumbled big boulders were lichen-covered and surrounded by all kinds of shining green plants and bright, tiny flowers. Snow buntings[4] flew in and out of all the crannies and the busy red mice[5] scurried into round little holes in the green moss. The two girls clambered over the rocks, stepping back and forth over the little streams. The poke was beginning to fill; the nunivak for winter sour greens went into it. Two other kinds, with flat, round leaves[6], went into their mouths.

Halfway up the mountain, Tokoya sat down on a rocky shelf and leaned the poke up against a rock. Ega was stooping over a patch of little fuzzy pink blossoms.[7] She held one up to Tokoya's nose. "It smells good." She sat with the flower cupped in her hands, sniffing it, smiling at Tokoya. "This is the only kind that smells so good."

"But here is the one which *looks* fine." Tokoya held up a lacy white cluster atop a slender stem.[8] "And its leaves taste good, too." From the base of the plant she pulled a scalloped round leaf and slipped it into her mouth. "Look down at our village; the houses are very small."

"And the people look like sandpipers." They both laughed; it was so comfortable, here among mossy rocks, greens and flowers, looking down to the cluster of mounds which was the village, where their neighbors were all outdoors, moving about like tiny dream figures.

The lake at the foot of the mountain was very blue; little black flecks floated on its glass—old-squaws, eiders and sandpipers. The jaegers still floated about, quiet and determined, and up the slopes and all about the two girls, the snow buntings fluttered and chirped and perched fearlessly near. Over all there was the warm sunshine, not a breeze stirring.

Tokoya eyed a little mound just below them, threw a pebble at it. Out popped a ground squirrel's[9] angry face. "Sikkik, sikkik," he scolded.

Ega laughed. "Sikkik, how angry you are. Can't you let us say a word to you? Come on out, then, and gather your plants for winter. We are going to the top of the mountain."

The top of the mountain was a green and blue and pink garden, set with enormous boulders all over its flat top. Tokoya left the poke and they roamed on aimlessly, picking the tiny gentians[10] to look at their queer green-blue petals, peering into dark crannies in the rocks, hoping to find a nest of young birds, gazing off over stretches of gold and green tundra, past Powuk, the great inland peak, to the eastern shore of the island and the queer, pointed brown mountains of Sevuokuk's other side.

Tokoya raised her arm and pointed straight across the north end of the island. "Over there lies Kukulik; I wonder how all Koonooku's people are. Soon they should be coming around in their boats to visit."

Ega shaded her eyes and searched the shore line, but cape after cape stood out along that north coast; many boats could be coming and still be hidden from view. Ega laughed suddenly. "One can easily see from here why the Kukulik people sing, "Alangaah, ah,"[11] when they are coming over here—

always another point in the way. Let us go back to the other side and see some more of the world."

It seemed to Ega the sun had never been so warm. On the west edge of the plateau they found such soft moss and grass in the spaces between the rocks. They pulled off their feather parkas and lay down in one of these mossy nooks, the sun beating down on their naked backs. Ega reached into her boot-top and pulled out a strip of dried mukluk and they lay there, propped up on their elbows, chewing slowly. Tokoya looked over at Ega and laughed softly and wriggled deeper into the moss.

Ega swallowed the last of her meat, reached out her arm and pulled off some green berries of the ground vine[12] and lay munching them and watching a longspur teetering on a tiny plant just beyond her reach. She studied his chestnut and black and white suit and wished she could have clothes as pretty; she watched his throat swell as he sang his quick little song over and over, and flipped suddenly away to the top of a big rock. Tokoya was looking down the mountainside to the beach, far below them. "Look," she pointed, "the water is so blue, and where there are big rocks in it, it is green. We can see the rocks far under the water, today, and there is no surf at all. The ocean is asleep."

The ocean was asleep. Flat as the lake, bluer than the clear blue sky, so quiet that even the cormorants and puffins and sea gulls seemed to feel it. They flew quietly by to the black cliff. There was hardly a bird cry now, only the faint squeaking of auklets in their holes in the rocky shore. Tokoya closed her eyes; it was so still and warm. She opened her eyes again and looked out across the deep blue to the dazzling white mountains of the old land to the west. High and white and carved in tall spires and towers, and so close they seemed, today! "I think we could jump into an ungiak and paddle over there before dark," said Tokoya.

"Oh-ee," moaned Ega, "I would be too sleepy." She closed her eyes; the bird voices grew fainter, there was no sound anywhere; the moss was soft. She slept.

Tokoya slept too, but the moment she woke she raised her head and looked out to sea. Had she dreamed that she must look out there? Was she still dreaming that two ungiaks were out there on that blue water?

"Ega, wake up and look quickly." Ega muttered and stirred and pushed her braids off her face. "Ah-ee! Ungiaks, two of them!"

She sat up quickly and reached for her parka. "Let us hurry. It must be Apangalook's brother from the old land. He was to come again this summer. Perhaps we can get down to the village before they land."

"No, wait a little," Tokoya said in a very small voice.

"What ails you? Don't you want to greet your relatives and hear all the news? And we must help with the food."

Tokoya sat, elbows on knees, and kept on watching the two large ungiaks. "These boats look strange."

Ega's round face became solemn. She sat down, too, and silently they watched the two boats draw near the shore in front of the village. And then they saw all the men of the village, in a solid body, walking down to the shore. Tokoya squeezed Ega's arm fiercely. At the head of that group were several, eight or ten, who looked twice as large as men. They were wearing the walrus-hide armor! Tokoya pointed farther down the beach. All the small ungiaks were in. That meant that their husbands were home and, no doubt, were among those men marching to the shore. They saw their men lift the big ungiaks, the whale boats, from their racks and lay them on their sides and crouch behind them.

The two strange boats were beached and more than two boat crews jumped out of them. The faint sound of strange shouts came up to the mountain. And then they saw one of the strangers start up the shore and crouch as though to shoot with a bow, but he toppled over and lay on the shore, half in the water. His companions were running up toward the boats; there were shouts and screams and thudding sounds.

The two girls lay over a big flat rock, clinging to each other, straining to see. The flame was all gone from Ega's cheeks and Tokoya's lips were trembling. If those strangers won out! If they killed all their men and took possession of the village, the women and children, what then?

Tokoya wished this could be just a dream, dreamed in their little mossy place up here, but she was afraid it was real, Massiu's dream come true. And while all the other women of the village hid in the darkest corners of the houses down there, she and Ega must stay up here and see it all.

Two more of the strangers sank to the sand, three more; they had not reached the overturned boats yet. It seemed to the two on the mountain that all the men behind the boats were still alive, but they could not be sure. Down went two more strangers. Brave they were, to rush up in plain view like that. Only five were left when they finally reached the boats, and there, all was a jumble and confusion and no one could tell what was happening. What misery, to be able to *see,* yet not really see what was taking place! Speechless and stiff, they lay there, it seemed a long time.

"Wo-ho-ho—ho, ho." Suddenly it came to their straining ears, the shout of triumphant Sevuokuk hunters! "Wo-ho-ho," and the girls saw people running from every house, heard all sorts of cries and noises.

Tokoya had never gone down the mountain so fast before; they almost forgot the poke of greens. Holding hands, bounding from rock to rock, sliding down over the drifts, frantically they raced.

Before they had quite reached the lake, they saw two tall figures coming out toward them from the village. The new husbands, still alive!

Massiu had dreamed a true dream, but his village had been ready!

· PALEHVEK ·
Moon of Plants Withering

CHAPTER XVII

Ungiakpuk

THE HOUSES were all opened to sun and wind for the summer airing. All the people had moved into their walrus-hide topeks.

For a good many days, during rain and storm, the women had sat inside, working up all the skins into clothes for winter. They had plenty to do.

Now the rain had stopped and the sun was peering through the clouds now and then. Far out over the water the fog hung like a curtain; the mountains of the old land were hidden.

Assoonga and all her neighbors sat before her tent, skins and furs and work boxes spread about them. Sekwo and the other children sat in a ring, playing the duck game, and Sekwo was having good luck. She gathered up all the little ivory ducks she could hold in one fist, threw them with a big fling into the middle of the ring. "Ah-ee—three of mine are alive."

She picked up three ducks which had landed upright. The others lay on their sides, dead. Dead like the stranger Inuit who had tried to take possession of Sevuokuk. Sekwo and the others looked silently at the dead ducks for a moment, remembering that day. But now the grown people must think that Massiu's warnings had been fulfilled, and that there was no more danger, for Apangalook and many others had gone away to the big lagoon to the south, to catch the fine pink-meated fish which lived in the big stream there, and here sat all the mothers and sisters, laughing and talking over their sewing. Sekwo threw down the ducks and crawled over to Assoonga's knee to watch her new cormorant-skin parka taking shape.

A whole pile of tanned cormorant skins lay beside Assoonga, but she was sewing them together pretty fast, all her stitches close to the feathers so they would not show, her needle flashing out from her, then toward her, swiftly.

129

Anatoonga and Okoma were both working on a parka of murre skins which Yahoh would wear over his cormorant-skin parka. The needle-like murre feathers would not then prick through to his skin when they got old.

Anatoonga looked across at Assoonga's flying fingers. "Ah, you are a swift needlewoman. I believe you will have that parka done before the sun goes into the ocean."

Assoonga laughed. They all knew very well no one could sew as fast as Anatoonga. Old Yokho spoke up. "Ahk, my daughter is a poor needle-woman; none of our family can make clothes fit to wear, but the menfolk must be covered somehow for the hunting."

The compliments flew back and forth; in their hearts they all knew that every one of them could turn out clothing fit for the hardest day on the ice.

Yokho chewed away on a mukluk boot sole, turning up the toe. Her old teeth were still pretty good. Between chewings she kept them all laughing. "Come, Tokoya, no need to look so worried. We all know this is the first snowshirt you have made for a husband. Remember to sew your seams on the outside; don't make a woman out of poor Kulukhon."

Tokoya hid her face but kept on intently cutting with her small oolak. From the white roll of split, cured intestine she was cutting strips the length of a snowshirt, and other strips for sleeves and for a hood. Beside her, Ega was preparing baby-seal hair tufts for trimming. The baby sealskin with its fuzzy white hair had been boiled for days in urine with pieces of the red bark from over the sea. Very valuable that bark was to needlewomen, for it gave seal hair and skin such a fine red color.[1]

Now the skin was soft, and Ega was twisting the red hair off in tufts and sewing them to a strip of tanned sealskin. Tokoya would need a strip around the bottom of Kulukhon's snowshirt, and Ega would need a strip three feet long to fasten to the back of her own snow parka which lay beside her, almost finished. To the end of that strip she would sew three small strips of intestine leather which she had dyed in the blood of Tatoowi, who was always having nosebleeds. She and Tatoowi both hoped that this use of his blood would stop his trouble. Carefully, with small stitches, Ega fastened these little pieces on the long "tail" of her snowshirt.

Now Wohtillin's plump Rohltungu was holding up the ceremonial snow-shirt she was just finishing and everyone stopped to look. This would be Wohtillin's costume for all the ceremonies, and a fine work she had done on it.

Of course it was made from small intestine of mukluk seal; this was the

whitest when it was scraped and blown and frozen. Rohltungu had prepared it during the coldest part of the winter, when she was sure it could
not suddenly thaw and be ruined. The strips were white as snow, and sewed
together with fine stitches, round and round instead of up and down, with
seams on the outside, and all along every seam, on body and sleeves and
hood, were the decorations.

All spring and summer Rohltungu had been saving the crests and beaks of
auklets and now, there they were, three of the brilliant orange and black
pieces in each tuft, and the tufts quite close together so that the whole
snowshirt was fairly covered. Yokho pointed down at her own old rain
parka of large-intestine of walrus. Thick and strong it was, but all wrinkled
and with no decoration. "Looks not much like mine, does it?" she laughed.
They all looked from the beautiful ceremonial shirt to Yokho's old one and
laughed aloud.

They were still laughing when a loud shout came from the beach below;
Sekwo and her friends were already running. Skins and knives spilled all
about as the women all jumped, too, and ran. That shout had something in
it!

Down at the shore stood what men were left in the village. They had been
helping or watching Timkaroo and Toozak put the last lashings in a new
ungiak. Now they were standing as though frozen, looking out to sea.
Behind them, the women and children also came to a standstill, wide-eyed.

Floating out there on the calm gray water, looming out of the gray fog
curtain, was such a thing as Inuit eyes could hardly bear to look at—a boat
so large, so tall, with such sails and masts reaching up into the fog that to
little Sekwo it seemed all the village, all the houses and meat racks and
boats, could be loaded into it.

Massiu was the first to get his voice: "Perhaps *this* was my dream."

Toozak pulled his eyes away from the terrible thing, looked at his
mother, at old Yokho who held Sekwo tightly by the hand, at Okoma
whose cheeks had no pink of tundra flowers in them now. Yokho leaned
forward stiffly, shading her old eyes with a wrinkled hand. The rest stood as
in a dream, eyes traveling from Yokho to the unbelievable thing out there
on the quiet water of their own cove. Yokho spoke in a harsh whisper as
though talking to herself or to spirits long gone. "This is the thing my
grandfather told of, that happened in *his* grandfather's time. Always I
thought it might be only a sorcerer's story. They told that in that time came
Ungiakpuk as tall as the Cape Mountain, that out of them came ungiak like

those of Inuit, that out of these landed tall Inuit whose skins were like snow, and who wore strange clothes. The people ran to the mountain and hid, and after a while, the strange ones went back to the Ungiakpuk and sailed away. My grandfather said this was so, but we could hardly believe— now I see."

She turned suddenly to Massiu. "And to the mountain *we* must go, too." Now she was her busy self again.

Massiu still looked out through the fog. "I cannot say this is an enemy, but something so strange is it that it is best we go to the great rocks. And go now; take only some food in small pokes."

His words released them. Everyone ran. The women snatched up the new clothing. The young men pulled pieces of drying mukluk off the racks and threw them into pokes and in no time at all they were all running past the lake, to the blessed mountain.

Massiu was the leader and set a steady trot. The children ran close beside their mothers, and old Yokho hobbled along as fast as anyone, Toozak beside her. In the midst of his racing thoughts, he heard her mutter as she trotted along, "Never did I think Yokho would live to see such happenings. One never knows what the spirits are sending next."

At the base of the mountain they turned a moment. The ship was still far out but growing taller and more awful each moment. Massiu spoke comfortingly. "They are still so far away I do not think they can see us yet, whatever kind of Inuit are in that boat."

But he did not hesitate to plunge up toward the rock jumbles and caves and crevices at the mountain's top. There was only the sound of quick, heavy breathing and the rattle of a pebble now and then as they scrambled up.

Once on top Massiu strode straight to a tall mass of broken rock, overlooking the village and the sea, and behind this they all crouched, gasping, women and children down in the crevices and half-caves, men just behind the big rocks above. Toozak helped Yokho down into a little niche, and she dropped her head on her knees. "Such doings for a poor old grandmother," she wheezed. "Where is the boat of giants, now?"

Toozak answered her from the top of the rock. "She is not far from our shore now, and, ah-eee—now there are small boats like our big ungiaks coming off her sides, and men dropping into them—" His voice died away; he could only look on the scene down there. His hands were aching from gripping so hard the edge of the big rock behind which he leaned. His heart was pounding in his ears. It seemed he could hear the hearts of all of them, beating in horror.

Yet they must keep on looking. Even Sekwo found a crack through which to peer, and Kaka squeezed in beside her.

There they came, those two calves of a big whale, nearer and nearer, then riding up on Sevuokuk shore and spilling out men, as many as two boat crews in whaling time. Sekwo squeezed a bit closer to Kaka—to Kaka with whom she was usually squabbling. The men were walking up to the village. "Keep your heads down," murmured Massiu. "Look only through the cracks."

Tokoya pressed her face to a tiny crack between rocks, the sharp edges dug into her ankles but she could not move. She watched the strange men walking about among the houses and did not know whether to be glad or sorry Kulukhon was gone to the lagoon.

Old Yokho was unbeatable. She had crawled painfully over to the edge and found a crevice to peer through. "A giant boat," she whispered to Massiu, "but these creatures do not seem to be giants."

"That is true, wise woman," answered Massiu. "They are larger than Inuit, but only a little, and I thought they would be giants like the one the people tell about, who left the hollow in the big rock back here on the mountain, when he sat down to rest. And look, they do not seem to be doing anything, only standing there."

Sure enough, the queer large strangers had walked all about the houses and now stood in a group on the beach, waving their arms about. In a moment, they went back down to their boats and, making queer, swaying motions with their paddles, went back to the big boat. As nearly as hiding ones could see, they carried nothing out of the houses, took nothing with them. This was very strange. What *did* they come for, then? And would the big boat go away now?

Massiu and Yokho both fell to chanting prayers and formulas in low trembling voices.

All day long the awful boat floated out there on the water, seemingly in the same spot, and that seemed magic, too, and all day long Massiu and his frightened ones stayed up on the mountain, wondering and praying.

They made themselves as comfortable as they could in the rocks after a while; they ate a little dried meat, and the children finally slept. Yokho slept fitfully, too, waking now and then to join Massiu in his low singing.

Toozak made himself look away, over to Powuk and the other inland peaks, and at the birds sailing about so ignorantly. Then, he would have to look back out over the water, and yes, the fearsome tall thing would still be there—no dream. He looked down. In the niche at his feet crouched Okoma, and she looked up into his eyes, forgetting all her manners, and Toozak gazed right back into hers, and saw all that she would say to him. "If we live, we two, surely in all the years to come, we shall never live through a stranger day than this one."

Just as the sun was sliding low behind the fog bank and the rocks were darkening and a cold breeze was coming over the mountain top, one small boat slid away from the big one and again came to shore. What, oh what, were those tall ones coming to do now?

Every pair of eyes strained through the cracks and peepholes. They saw the same very tame doings as in the morning. Those people walked around, went into the houses, came out again. In a little while the boat was going out toward the big one again, and the watchers breathed a long breath.

In a few moments, Toozak nudged Timkaroo. "Look, is it not moving?"

Slowly, like a great ghost in the dusk, the strange thing was drawing farther into the fog, farther and farther from shore, dimmer and dimmer in the dusk and in the fog. At last they were all squinting and straining for a last view of it. It was gone.

It was gone, and there were they, alone on their mountain top, safe. It had been the strangest day of all their lives.

They knew it was not a dream.

Not a dream, either, Okoma's soft little nose against Toozak's in the dusk. In this moment of deliverance from they knew not what, all ordinary manners could be forgotten! And in Toozak's brain, the great excitement of the strange visitors was somehow drowned out in the thought, "Will Apangalook let me begin working for a wife now?"

Hand in hand in the soft good dark, he and Okoma began finding their way down the mountain.

·AKOMAK·
Moon of Sitting

CHAPTER XVIII

In the Storm

THERE was simply whiteness over all the world; ice on the sea and snow on the land, the north wind sweeping straight down from the top of the world, howling to be let through the narrow strait, and bursting with released loud fury upon the Island, filling the air with snow, pushing the ice pack closer and closer upon Sevuokuk's shores, ice-coated shores where the slush ice formed and thickened and pushed out toward the pack.

In all the white swirl and clamor only one dark object—Toozak, of course, that young eager one, facing the storm in hope of getting some birds, which on such a day would be sweeping in close under the cliffs to escape the wind.

Toozak had been out all day and had tramped many miles along that slippery beach. Once, a little flock of guillemots[1] who had forgotten to go south came squeaking toward him out of the foam of the storm. He had quickly cast his bolas into the flock. The wind made casting difficult but he caught one of the tiny things, and, once through a rift in the flying snow, he had glimpsed something on the ice a few feet from shore and added two petrels[2] and a murre[3] to his catch. Foolish ones, they had feasted through the autumn until they were too fat to get off the water and the ice had come down upon them. Now they were easy prey to a nimble boy who, with a long stick, could reach out and poke them in close enough to reach. Grasping the birds by the neck, Toozak held them up before him, "Ah, you foolish ones—now you must be eaten."

He bit each one quickly in the back of the head; they were soon dead. Tying their necks together with a piece of seal-hide thong, Toozak slung the birds over his shoulder and marched on.

Toozak was dressed for hunting, with cormorant-skin parka, feather side in, covered with reindeer-skin parka, fur side out, with sealskin trousers, with fawnskin socks and sealskin boots. Yet the storm was beginning to bite through all this. He pulled his head into his hood as far as he could and stamped his boots hard as he tramped along. All of a sudden the wind swirled from around a big boulder and flung a mixture of sand and snow into his eyes.

Toozak blinked and shook his head and bent still lower. "This is no place to be now. Perhaps this is going to be one of those storms whose power flattens Inuit into four-legged crawling things."

Akomak, sure enough—the moon when the sun rose over the same inland peak day after day, and the darkness crept in early. Already sea and land and sky were one moving, howling grayness, bitter cold; the light had gone.

If it were not for that girl, that shining-eyed Okoma, he would not be out on such a day as this. All the sensible hunters were beside the ningloo lamps today, carving harpoon heads or bird darts. Timkaroo would laugh at him if he could see him out here, but Timkaroo had won his Ega now; he could laugh at his young brother for being in such a hurry. But that was the soul Toozak had been given—if there were a thing to be done, he must do it in a hurry. The more food and skins he brought in to Yahoh's house, the sooner would come the night when Okoma would be quiet when he went to her sleeping place; the sooner could they go back to his father's house, back to the big house of Apangalook, where Toozak belonged.

Toozak's legs were like sodden driftwood. He could barely push along into the shrieking force of that north wind. He was not sure how many hours he had been out, nor how far he had tramped along the beach; sometimes he wondered if he were lost, yet he knew he was still on the beach, there was sand stinging his cheeks as well as snow, and he felt there was higher land at his right hand. But it was all one darkness now. Were his legs still moving ahead, or were they just going up and down, up and down, in a bad dream? He could not keep his eyes open and his brain was numb. Now—was he a real Inuit hunter or not? Would all the hours and days and months of running the circle, of lifting rocks and jumping over them, and running trapline, save him? Ah-ee, never, not even on that first day on the ice that seemed so very long ago, had he been so tired. It was no use; north wind was winning today.

Toozak dropped to hands and knees, crawled along, so slowly, the murres and fulmars dragging in front from his shoulders. The rocks of the beach dug through boots and trousers, into his knees, the wind shrieked louder and louder, the air was so full of flying sand and snow that Toozak choked; his breath pushed back into his throat. Ah, that Okoma—maybe he would never—he set his teeth, made his sore knees keep going. Okoma liked bird-skin clothes; perhaps Anatoonga would let her have these skins if Toozak the foolish one ever got in with them. Surely he had passed the village by now; Yahoh's house was at this end. Swoosh! Another swirl of snow and sand in his face—and there was a small black hole in front of him; he tumbled in, into sudden windlessness, quiet. He was in Yahoh's house entrance, and he lay there, breathing hard.

After a while Toozak began to feel alive again; he picked up a snow beater which had once been part of a walrus rib, and began to beat the snow and ice from boots and parka. He tried to be quiet, for he could hear Yahoh's voice. He was telling a story. One thing Yahoh did do well, and that was tell a story. Now came Anatoonga from her lamp in the far corner, opened her eyes wide at sight of that weary, drooping hunter, lifted his parkas quickly and peeled both off in one motion, over his head. "Ah, boy, a bad day outside for hunters, is it not? A good day inside for story telling."

Anatoonga was all in favor of this son-in-law of hers. She had lived long enough with a poor hunter to appreciate a good provider when she saw one, and now she had all the meat and oil and skins she had so long dreamed of having, like the other women of the village. She soon had Toozak's trousers and boots off, shaken, turned inside out, hung over the rack to dry, and Toozak was wriggling his bare shoulders in comfort; it was something, to be waited upon as a real provider; he climbed onto the furs of his sleeping place and lay back, relaxed and listening. The family were all there, and Kaka and Sekwo, those two quarreling playmates, too. They had come to spend the stormy day at Yahoh's; they knew there would be story telling there.

And yes, Okoma, of course, busy with the seal Toozak had netted at the cape before the storm, but she must not look at him now. Everyone was very quiet; only Yahoh's voice, telling the story of the creation of man by an ant and a spider.

In the beginning when these creatures were to create man they made plans about the shape of man. The spider would shape his man with the mouth on the breast and the breast on the place where our cheek is. He also added that man must live forever.

When the spider stopped talking, the ant began to talk. His plan was a bad one. He wished to make us as we are now. Also he told the spider that it would be nice for the people if they had death. These creatures talked for a long time. At last the spider gave up his plan and followed the ant's bad plan. Now, when an ant is seen by anyone, it is always thrown into burning fire on account of its bad plan. When a person sees a spider he always throws small pieces of any kind of food to it and pretends to feed it. They do this for the spider's mercifulness. The name of the spider, Apayapyeek, means almost the same as Grandfather, Apa.

"Grandfather, spider, eh?" Kaka and Sekwo chuckled. Lying on their stomachs on the furs of the sleeping place behind Yahoh, they were playing a lazy game. Ivory ducks and geese were sailing down little channels in the fur, but the ningloo was so nice and warm, with two lamps going, that these young ones sometimes nearly fell asleep as the stories went on.

Toozak sat up and began to work on his bird dart. Had he really been near death, out in that storm? He felt well, and warm and happy, now. He balanced the five-foot shaft of a straight piece of driftwood over his fingers. It was finished, hewn and shaped, round and smooth and light in the hand. Into its end he began lashing the dart socket of walrus bone into which the ivory dart would be fitted. He sat cross-legged, scraping a strip of whalebone with his stone knife. Long hours it would take to scrape and shave the baleen into quarter-inch strips thin enough to lash the socket tight into the split end of the shaft, but there was plenty of time, and how pleasant this was, sitting with the family in warmth and comfort, while that north wind howled over the roof!

Sekwo held up one of her ivory toys. "White whale, little whale. Can you tell a story about him, Yahoh?"

Yahoh felt the edge of his stone knife, his round face smiling, picked up a piece of ivory for a bucket handle.

Ah yes, the white whale was once an old woman. She lived with her grandson who was blind. They lived on mice which the old woman snared or killed with a small bow and arrow. The boy had a larger bow which was large enough to kill larger game. One day the old woman went out and in a moment rushed back in calling her grandson, saying, "Grandson, prepare your bow and arrows, for the bear and her two cubs are coming along."

The boy answered and said, "How would I kill them for I can see nothing?"

But the old woman answered, "I will tell you to let the arrow go when the bears are at your point of aim."

So the boy prepared his bow and arrows and went out. He sat in front of the house and took aim in the direction where the bears were going to pass. When the bear came to the place at which the boy was aiming the old woman told him to let the arrow go, which he did, and at once killed the mother bear. She told him to shoot the cubs too. He killed all of them without seeing them, and the old woman did not tell him he had killed them. She told him to go into the house for she was going to get some dry plants for their fire.

Yahoh paused and held the ivory handle to the light, squinted along it, traced a careful ellipse on one side. Everyone waited in silence.

When the boy entered the house the old woman skinned the bears and cut up the meat. When it was cut up she hung most of it to dry on the meat rack. As soon as she entered the house, the boy went out and crawled off for some plants to eat. His grandmother boiled the bear meat, also some mice.

The boy crawled off for some distance. While he was crawling, a snipe sat before him and ate the plants for which he was feeling. When the snipe had done this for the third time, the boy became angry and told it to go away.

The snipe began to talk, saying, "I was coming to help you out but you tell me to depart."

The boy then replied in kind words, telling the snipe he would not speak that way again. Then the snipe sat in front of him and began to lick his eyes with her tongue for a while. After a time, she told the boy to open his eyes. The boy tried to open his eyes but his eyes could see just a little. The boy told the snipe he did not see anything.

The snipe continued licking and again told him to open his eyes. The boy did so and saw it was light. His sight was like our sight and he could see as far as we can see. The boy then said, "Now I can see just a little for my eyes are open only at the corners."

The snipe licked them again and told him to look again. When the boy opened his eyes, he was astonished, for now he could see the tiniest insect that lived in the depths of the sea. He told the snipe that he could see clearly. The snipe then told him to go home and to shut his eyes as usual when he entered the house. She told him that he had killed all the bears and that his grandmother had planned to let him have only mice to eat.

The boy went home with his eyes open.

When the house was in sight he saw the rack loaded with meat to dry as well as some hanging over the house. As soon as he came near the house, he shut his eyes. When he was in the house he smelled the odor of bear meat. He said to his grandmother, "Where does all this smell come from?"

The old woman answered in anger, "Do you think some beasts you shot are in here?"

The boy answered, "Do you think you could kill them if you were blind?"

Then he asked for his meat. The old woman put a dish of boiled mice in front of him and served bear meat for herself. As they began to eat the boy kept his eyes closed. After a few minutes, he opened one of his eyes and saw his grandmother eating bear cub meat, which is tender. Suddenly the boy stood up and grabbed his grandmother by the hand and pulled her onto the walrus skin which was spread on the platform. She asked him to eat bear meat with her, but he wrapped her up in the walrus skin and dragged her to the shore and threw her into the water.

When she came up she was changed to a white whale. She asked for her sewing things and the boy threw everything that she called for into the water. She has worn the form of a white whale to this day.

When we kill a white whale we look in the brain. In the brain a single human hair is found which is grey, so people believe that the white whale was once an old woman.

It was very quiet in the ningloo. All were thinking about the old woman who had to become a white whale. Yahoh's bucket handle was nearly finished. Kaka was hanging half over the platform, watching. Yahoh was short and chunky, and he was the lazy one, but he had the smartest fingers of them all when he wanted to use them. His stone knife bit into the ivory. Kaka's eyes were round and intent as he watched the clever stone edge trace graceful curving lines on the ivory, curving lines one inside the other, lines that were almost round, like eyes. Kaka was already trying these things himself.

Anatoonga looked up from her sewing, looked around at all her family. She turned and trimmed the lamps, pressing the moss down evenly all along the edges. The light came clear and strong, shone on all the busy faces around the platform, on gleaming shoulders and arms and breasts. With two lamps going in the ningloo, no one need be encumbered by clothes, at all.

"Perhaps people should have food, soon," said Anatoonga. Okoma quickly rolled her sealskin up, and went out into the cooking place.

In a little while, they all sat on the floor about the great wooden platter which was full of boiled birds and blubber and broth. Anatoonga with her oolak had cut meat and blubber into convenient pieces and everyone could reach in easily. The meat with blubber was good; some nunivak with it made it even better; they all smacked their lips and laughed, for no reason, just that everything was good. With two fingers together, each one scooped up the good broth from the bottom of the platter; it went fine. Toozak suddenly had never felt better; something was tingling inside him.

Pretty soon the family would all be lying in the furs on the platform, to rest and sleep as long as they liked. Toozak listened—the north wind was still screaming above them; it might go on perhaps for days, sweeping over and possessing the island, as it had done through all the long ages gone, ever since Inuit had first come to Sevuokuk, and long before. Toozak sat dreamily, a piece of boiled auklet forgotten in his hand, his head tilted back, listening to the storm, thinking of those long-ago people. The house of Yahoh must by now be only a little rounded mound on the beach—the wind would be sweeping the snow warmly all over it.

. . . . .

Darkness and silence in the house of Yahoh. The family were all asleep now, lying across the platforms each in his own place, feet toward the center of the house. Toozak, though, was not asleep. He raised himself on an elbow. Young Kaka, beside him, was really sleeping the deep sleep of boyhood; it had been too stormy for him or Sekwo to go home tonight. Yahoh was snoring regularly beside his sweet-faced Anatoonga. All the faces looked so peaceful and kind in the fitful glow of the one lamp left burning very low. Toozak hoped that Anatoonga would not waken just now and call to Okoma to trim the lamp, as she often did. He slid out of his robes, pulled out a pair of birdskin moccasins and stepped into them. Looking once more at the sleeping faces, he started a slow journey across the ningloo in this special soundless footwear of young lovers.

Okoma lay very still, an arm thrown across her forehead, but Toozak wondered if she really were asleep. He knelt close to the platform, watching her mouth, lifted the skins of her sleeping robe a bit and put one knee up on the platform as though to climb up.

Okoma sat up. The thing was not so easily to be done! He put his hands on her shoulders but she twisted and turned in his grasp; she was worse than a young seal to hold onto.

Then came the voice of Anatoonga. "What is this? Do weary ones have to be wakened from good sleep by some foolishness of young people?"

Toozak slid down and crept quickly back to his own place. Yet he did not feel so badly. There would of course have to be many such encounters before she would be quiet, but it seemed to him she had not been really angry at all!

CHAPTER XIX

Those Two

THE NORTH WIND had brought the ice, and gone whispering away again. Toozak had almost forgotten how fierce the wind had blown on that awful day. It was quiet again, and cold, and on the ice were walrus and seals. The hunters were out every day.

Quiet, too, in the house of Yahoh. Oh yes, Yahoh was there! A man should not be expected to go out to that hard work *every* day. Besides, Toozak would bring something in; he never came empty-handed at night. He had even brought in a fine ribbon seal the day before, and it was understood of course that Okoma was to have the skin for a clothes bag.

Yahoh squinted at the new ivory comb he was making for Anatoonga, and glanced at his busy daughter, sitting on the floor with the big seal in front of her, her shining black head bent over it, her cheeks very bright, her eyes so intent and serious. Her father could see why Toozak or any hunter would work to own such a girl. And Yahoh, lazy man that he was, was not so bad in some ways; he thought he knew what his duty as a father was.

Okoma would have a clothes bag as fine as Ega's, but for a clothes bag the seal must be skinned through the mouth, just as for a poke, so Anatoonga must sit near, to help with some advice now and then.

Okoma had skinned inside the lips and was working up toward the eyes, under the skin. The muscles of her bare arms moved and rippled, as her small oolak worked around under there, and her face was very still, as though listening. She felt the oolak move against the eye socket. Carefully she loosened the skin from the socket and moved on up, cutting, cutting, until she felt the ears and cut them loose, very close to the skull. Now the whole head skin was loose. She looked up at Anatoonga, who smiled, "You are doing well; you have not cut through eyelids or ears. Now go on to the

145

flippers; break the joint and leave the bone in. You will have a fine skin without holes."

Okoma's round little arm was reaching up under the skin as far as she could push it, her oolak moving swiftly around, cutting deep into the blubber, leaving a thick layer of it on the skin. At last she sighed and straightened her back. "Ah-h—will you help me now, Anatoonga?"

Anatoonga knelt at the rear end of the seal and took firm hold of the rear flippers. Now Okoma began pushing the skin of the seal's skull back, back, over the head. Then, she took hold of the skull and pulled. Slowly the gleaming fat body began sliding out through the little opening. It had to slide out, what with Okoma squeezing and pulling, and Anatoonga pulling back on the skin!

Finally Okoma's seal lay there, eyes black in a body of white fat. Anatoonga lifted him and carried him out into the passage, to cut him up for food.

Now Okoma had a satisfied look. Turning the skin inside out was pure pleasure. Very soon she was sitting with the skin spread before her, cutting off with her oolak all the blubber she could, and dropping the chunks into a big clay pot. There in the warmth of the house they would render out into delicious seal oil.

Now she was scraping and scraping, with regular strokes of her cup-shaped ivory blubber scraper; when the little cup was full of oil and fat she emptied it into the pot too. This part of it she had known how to do since she was a small girl.

In Yahoh's hands the new ivory comb was taking shape. From his oval wooden tool box he now selected a blade of stone with such a fine edge that he could etch hairlike lines in the ivory, short radiating lines, and tiny cross-lines. He bent over his work, wrist on knee, the piece held firmly in his left hand. He spoke softly, "Okoma, there are things a father must say to his daughter." Okoma bent lower over the sealskin.

"Many sleeps has a young man slept in this house. Many times also have young people wakened others from slumber in the night, with their wrestling. It is well now if they be quiet. The young man will sleep beside you many sleeps before he will try really to become your husband. Things have always been done this way by the people. It is time now for you to be quiet when he comes to you."

Okoma only nodded humbly and was very busy with the skin. Her lips twitched. Her happy soul was tugging at them, wanting them to smile. She had been wondering how long she would have to wait for her father to give her this order. A girl could never suggest to a father his duty. Okoma turned the seal again; she stroked the beautiful smooth skin fondly.

That night in the quiet dark, Okoma again heard the shuffle of birdskin moccasins. She moved over under her soft furs and closed her eyes and lay very still. In a moment she knew that someone knelt beside her, and the little happy soul was tugging at her lips again, to think how surprised that young man was going to be when she made no move to struggle with him. He might be surprised to know she had never really *wanted* to struggle, not with *him*, yet she could not, of course, have been so improper.

Toozak raised the edge of the skin covers, peered into Okoma's face. She was apparently sound asleep, yet, somehow, he doubted it. His heart leaped—had he at last come to the night when there would be no commotion in the ningloo? He slid in beside the quiet girl and lay very still, not touching her. Both were soon asleep—Toozak and his Okoma.

PART TWO
Being the Later Years

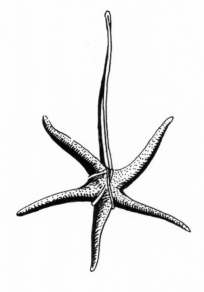

CHAPTER XX

Son of Toozak

THAT was a good year for Yahoh, the lazy one. He was not often seen out on the ice that winter, for that quick, laughing, young hunter who wanted Yahoh's daughter brought in plenty of seal and walrus to the house of Yahoh. When the withering time of plants came again, Toozak brought Okoma home to the house of his father. She was the wife of Toozak, the hunter.

And another circle of moons had turned themselves about the Island. Here it was Penahvek again, the end of another winter, the moon when the water begins to flow.

Assoonga stooped over her outdoor fire and stirred the big pot of walrus meat with a long, bone spoon. "A little tighter at this end, boy," she called to Toozak. She had to smile then, for Toozak, her merry one, for one moment was not smiling; his mother had to laugh for him. Babies came to Inuit all the time. This child Okoma was about to have for Toozak was not the first one Assoonga had helped into the world. Toozak frowned, and tugged at the thong attached to the walrus hide. Balancing up there on that driftwood frame, he tied the last corner, clambered down onto the foot rest, onto the ground, and gave his place to Tokoya and Ega who were to split the hide.

Tokoya lifted her tiny Lozama from off her shoulders and laid her on a deer skin beside the frame. Lozama was a beautiful baby, so full of smiling that Kulukhon and Tokoya could not feel too bad that their first one had not been a boy.

Assoonga spoke softly. "Split the skin as fast as your oolaks can travel. I think we shall soon need it."

Toozak hurried back up the beach, to the edge of the tundra, where

Apangalook and Timkaroo were lashing a small tent frame of driftwood sticks together.

Okoma sat beside the fire, her head bowed low—even on this mild, moist June morning she felt cold. She, Okoma, known as the liveliest, the quickest, in all the village, fit partner for that swift-moving, laughing Toozak, sat here like a great lump; and she was the cause of the hurry here this day. Assoonga was tasting the broth and looking sharply at her. "Your son is soon ready, eh, young woman?"

Okoma stood up awkwardly. Her tender young lips were blue. Slowly she walked up the beach to the edge of the tundra slope and sat down on a big flat rock. Ah-eee! She was tired! And some spirit of pain was rising to his knees within her young body.

Young and new to this she was, but she sat quietly on her rock, watching. Assoonga would see that all was done properly—there was no doubt of that. Her own mother Anatoonga would be coming, too, but Assoonga was the one who would order all things. Okoma saw her glance her way once again, and speak to the two busy young women on the frame and to the men. All began to move faster.

Tokoya and Ega climbed down. They had, with clever swift strokes, split the thickness of that great hide, leaving it still together at one edge, so that the hide was still one, but twice its first size. Now it was going over the new tent frame.

Over all the quick sounds of busy talk, for people always talk when they work together, the voices of Sekwo and Kaka floated down to Okoma from the mossy slope above her. They were gathering grass, dry grass, for the tent floor, but they had some playing to do, too. It was a balmy day for June; the sun shone over the low-hanging cloud bank and the wind blew softly from the south.

Okoma watched the lively Sekwo fling back her parka hood to let the warm spring wind blow over her laughing face. Shouting and squealing, she and Kaka rolled in the moss, threw handfuls of it at each other, sailed leaf ungiaks down the tiny streams finding their way to the beach from the snowdrifts above. They were finding this day a good one.

Okoma set her teeth, yet smiled at Sekwo's laughter. That girl was growing every day more like her brother Toozak. And Kaka, that sturdy round-eyed one! Perhaps someday she, Okoma, and Toozak, would have such a son, racing over the tundra, looking for fox dens, snaring lemmings, killing his first seal. Her thoughts for months had been a constant prayer that their first-born be a son. Carefully she had done all things to bring this about. From the very first she had eaten only the foods allowed pregnant women, so she would have a boy. From the very first she had had Assoonga say the regular prayers over her each morning. And how strongly Assoonga had chanted! How she had rubbed her, spitting in her hand, rubbing Okoma's stomach while she chanted. And Toozak—he had not cut his hair once since he first had the news, so that the child should surely be born alive and live long.

Okoma watched the sun, a red eye sinking now toward the band of fog far out there over the quiet gray water. The clouds of auklets were coming in toward the cliff, each to the warm shelter of his own tiny hole in the rocks. The cool moist breath of ocean whispered in from the sea and cooled the girl's wet brow; pain was insistent now. She rose and moved slowly up the beach.

Where the men had set up her little tent on the edge of the mossy slope, she gathered some dry heather and a few little sticks and began to cook her meal of broth in her own little clay pot. This night she must eat alone, of separate food.

At last, through the moist dusk Sekwo and Kaka came running, arms full of grass. "Ah-yah, Sekwo, I have a bigger load than you; let me in first."

Breathless and important they were, those two, spreading grass, gathering rocks and tying them to long pieces of walrus thong. Toozak came and flung the thongs over the tent. The cover would not blow off now if the wind came. Toozak had to push his long hair out of his eyes; he and the children all cast quick glances at Okoma, kneeling there by her tiny fire, but of course said nothing. Only Sekwo, a big rock hugged to her breast, stopped and regarded her with a bright eye. "You, girl," called Assoonga quickly, "go now and find some dry moss; we will want much of it. And you, Kaka, take Okoma's own small bucket and bring her fresh water from the little stream, and be sure you do not drink from that bucket yourself, lest some sickness come into you."

Toozak was restless that night. His thoughts were racing inside his head; they would not lie down and let him have peace. Curious and fearful he lay there, and always Okoma's little pointed face, drawn with pain, brightness gone from its eyes, floated there before his eyes. He tried to think of other things, of the day he got his first Ongtopuk, of the day he killed Nanook alone, of Walanga, trapped there in the passageway at Kukulik—all those carefree things of his boyhood, but the thoughts would not stay. His child—

would it be a boy?

He rolled over and tossed off his reindeer robe. Apangalook and Timkaroo were sleeping heavily at the other side of the summer topek. He knew he should be asleep, too. What was going on in the little topek up there was women's business; Assoonga would call him when they needed him. He felt glad that Walanga and his new wife had moved back over to Kukulik to her people; surely there were now no others in the village who felt spiteful toward him or Okoma, who would pray to the spirits to give her a hard time. They had been careful not to tell any but their nearest relatives that Okoma's time had come.

Sleep would not come. He crawled to the opening and peered out. After a while, there was Assoonga coming from the little topek. She smiled and beckoned. "You have a fine son. We are ready for the water now."

Now he could move again, do something! He hurried down through the deep, loose gravel to the quiet shore and dipped a seal-hide bucket carefully into the water! The sun's first rays were coloring the waves. He carried his bucket up to Assoonga, then stood waiting. In the topek was all sorts of soft, foolish talk of women. He heard Okoma laugh. She would not be so big-eyed and gray-faced as he had seen her last night. Then Toozak began to feel like his own gay self again; he shifted his feet restlessly. He knew Assoonga was washing the baby in the salt water he had brought, and wrapping him in a soft sealskin. With a piece of sinew, she had carefully tied the navel cord and with her own little stone oolak cut it. From the talk, he imagined that Anatoonga, excited and happy at assisting at the birth of her daughter's first child, a boy, was already making the baby's cap of skin from the head of a reindeer fawn, inside of which she would fasten a little strip of the navel cord Assoonga had cut off. When the cord itself dried and came off, Okoma would wear it on her belt.

At last Assoonga had put the walrus-intestine bag containing all the things pertaining to the birth back in the far corner of the topek where it must stay for five days before she could carry it away up the mountain-side. She came out. "Now Toozak, you may come."

There was Okoma, dressed in her kalevak, her thighs bound with a strip of deerskin, resting in a kneeling position, arms on a big bundle of skins. In this way had she gone through the hours of the night and just so must she remain for the five days of her staying in. She and Toozak both gazed at the plump sleeping baby and Toozak suddenly felt a great strong wave of feeling rushing through him.

"Assoonga's prayers were good, were they not?" He bent to loosen his bootstrings.

"And remember," said Assoonga, "keep them loose all the five days Okoma stays in here, so that the boy's voice will not be choked. He must be called Enook, for your uncle who left this world last summer."

Toozak nodded. This was right. The old uncle who had lived on the east side of the island; now his name-soul had a home again, and the baby's own soul now had a helper-soul, so all things should be well with him. Always there was someone going to the other world; always name-souls waiting for new bodies.

Yes, it was Assoonga who had to see that things were done as they should be in this village. Now there was another soul in the big house of Apanga-look, and that soul, a boy; a boy who would grow to be a hunter, a provider.

Always they must pray for boys to be born.

CHAPTER XXI

To the Lagoon

APANGALOOK'S FAMILY were going to the lagoon, and he did not have to tell them to hurry; they were all eager. Off came the topek covers; into the bottom of ungiak they went, all rolled up. In went deerskins and clothing bags, clay pots and bone tools, bags of mangona, bags of seal oil. Kaka and Sekwo were flipping up and down the beach like young foxes. Kaka was trying to carry everything. Apangalook might change his mind about taking a young cousin along if he did not show how useful he was! Sekwo handed him a bulging ribbon-seal clothes bag, "This is all—here come the women."

Timkaroo strode up to Ega. With one quick move, he tucked his head under her left breast, caught her above the knees with his arms, and tossing her over his shoulder, carried her thus through the low surf to the boat and rolled her into it. In the same way went the others, squealing. Assoonga held her precious cooking pots in her arms but got tossed in just the same way. When a man moves, no woman may dispute him. Kaka eyed Sekwo up and down—no, not just yet. Someday he would show her!

Here comes Okoma with little Enook, a squalling bundle of furs, off on his first journey. "Come, boy, hunters don't cry," says Toozak. "When another moon has turned his face, you will be big enough to ride on your mother's neck in the right way."

Here go Sekwo and Kaka; Timkaroo tosses them into the middle of the boat like puppies. "Ah-ee, ah-ee," they sing; the boat is sliding out from shore. The sun has burst through the fog; the island is green and gold and the water the bluest blue and the surf sparkles with light, and in Apangalook's big ungiak there is not a solemn face.

"Ah-ee, ah-ee," sing all the men at the paddles. Going to the lagoon! Best time of all the year!

Okoma is bright-eyed and smiling again. Toozak bends to his paddle with a shout, "Ay-ah-ee." Life is good again.

. . . . .

When the sun was sliding down toward the sea that evening the boat slid into a narrow channel on the north coast, and there lay the big lagoon inside, shining, inviting, its quiet water reflecting the white sand beach around it, and the green grassy slopes above it.

Every summer, when they slid through that narrow channel and came into the lagoon, Toozak felt the same excitement. Every time, he remembered the old people's stories of the first Inuit to come to Sevuokuk—of how their leader one day happened into this narrow place, and discovered the treasure they needed if they would keep alive in the new home. Both sides of the narrow channel were heaped with the finest driftwood Inuit could want—here were timbers for winter houses. Toozak knew the story well. It had been handed down through all the years. They built a good kind of house, for Inuit still lived in the same kind, half underground, with timbered walls pegged together with walrus bone, roofed with whale ribs and timbers covered with sod, a walrus-stomach window in the roof. There were remains of the old houses in many places, too. Toozak had explored around them when he was a boy, but grown people left the old homes of long-gone people alone, always.

But people still needed timbers for houses and boat keels and meat racks and sledges and many other things. Here were they, now, the family of Apangalook, come down all those years from the first people, here in the same lagoon, looking for the same things.

And that lagoon was a place to put anyone in fine spirits. They had barely set up the tent when Kaka and Sekwo came racing down the beach, laughing and screaming, "Look, look what we have found, and there are big ones, too, out in the lagoon, that cannot fly!"

They had each two or three goslings by the neck. And Toozak was still not too grown up for that sort of fun, either. Up and down the beach they ran, dodging and jumping and shouting, to catch those fuzzy squeaking things. The place was all astir; goslings cheeping frantically, sandpipers racing along the beach and keening in sympathy, and out in the lake, flightless ducks and geese, dozens of them, swimming up and down with anxious cries. Yes, they might have to be caught, too. Assoonga's fire was already blazing and the clay pot hung over it.

Hours later, when the sun's rays came flatly across tundra and lagoon, and a stillness had slid over the summer night, they were all seated on the fine sandy beach around the fire. The pot full of delicious goslings stood where all could reach in.

Kaka lay in the edge of the grass, propped on an elbow, a whole gosling in his hand. His white teeth tore off sizeable bites; there was juice all over his face and running down his arms. The air was still warm; a light breeze puffed the lagoon into rosy ripples. The others talked together in dreamy low voices, making plans for all that must be done. But Kaka merely rolled over on his back, holding a dripping gosling leg over his open mouth. Life could not be better than this.

Soon they would roll into deerskin robes and sleep awhile. But when the sun would be high again, the sandpipers and ducks and geese, calling, the small birds out on the tundra in the tiny willows, singing, the world all awake, people must be awake, too, and busy. Certain things must be done in this moon of plant gathering.

Certain things to be done. Yes. Their very lives depended on these things—timbers to repair the winter house, and food, always food. This was what Apangalook and Assoonga knew so well.

In the bright early morning light Kaka and Sekwo were racing over mossy hummocks, falling and rolling down the tiny soft slopes, peeking under each willow to find bird nests, now and then digging up a bit of willow root to chew on. It was doubtful whether they would get much real work done.

But Tokoya and Ega and Assoonga worked steadily. Soft green plants of nunivak were at their best in this moon, and calm sunny days do not come too often on Sevuokuk. It was so warm that Ega had on only her birdskin parka and the hood of that thrown back. Her face was flushed and serious, her black braids swinging as she stooped and knelt in the soft green patches. "These will be fine sour greens; after they have been in the seal poke under some good heavy stones for many sleeps, we can have greens with our meat."

The cries of the two children come from far across the tundra. "Those!" laughs Assoonga. "They are not working *too* hard. I think their poke will not be too full to carry!"

On the other side of their camp, there is the driftwood, treasure of all Inuit since the beginning.

Through how many years, from how many inland rivers of the great mainland to the east, floating, drifting, pushed by spring ice, tossed by ocean storms, moving ever on and on, these tall trees, roots, branches, fragments, were tossed up here and left to wait! And then Inuit came, and had need of Nature's gift.

Apangalook clambers all over the great pile, Kulukhon and Toozak behind him. When he, peering and poking, located a good timber, they were all ready to pry with sticks, to pull and tug until the chosen pieces were out and free on the beach. Then they held a log and watched Apangalook, the master axeman. Standing astride of the log, with steady care he starts a cleavage in the end; with quick sure strokes of his ivory axe he splits the log for a foot or so, then picks up one of his ivory wedges and pounds it into the crack. Kneeling first on one side of the log and then on the other, he works with axe and wedges until the whole log is split, straight and fine—two timbers for the winter house.

When they all sat down on a big log to rest, here came Sekwo running. Assoonga had given her an errand. She brought a whalebone bucket of clear water, some willow roots and a little bag in which were pieces of seal blubber. The water was best of all; they drank and drank. That Assoonga! She is always just as a woman should be, remembering the hard work of her men and thinking of their comfort.

Toozak munched away and gazed all about him. Always there was something good to see in the world. He looked across the calm lagoon, green bordered. Beyond it were the blended colors of "Nuna," the tundra, and the bright brown slopes of the big mountain, Powooiliak, in the southwest. He threw back his head, looking into the quiet sky. "Apangalook, look!" he cried. "The one who can sling with a bird sling is here."

"Yes, Klooyak it is." They all shaded their eyes and gazed up at the white gyrfalcon sailing about up there in the blue. Timkaroo laughed. "He knows he is safe with us. None of us wants to have harm come to him or become a poor hunter because of killing Klooyak. He can sail around up there and be safe and there are plenty of birds for him out on the tundra."

Toozak watched the big white bird shrink to a tiny spot in the far blue; he thought dreamily that it was a good sign, having Klooyak fly over them so close, and lifted another piece of blubber to his mouth. There was always a great good feeling in this place of the lagoon. In fact, Toozak's lips were curled up in a smile always these days—such a fine place in which to hunt, plenty of building material, plenty of food, and now there was the fine young son, too.

. . . . .

Okoma sat on the sand at the door of the topek, sewing. Her son slept on his bed of skins inside the tent, and Okoma hummed softly the ground squirrel song: "Sikki klunga, ah hunga, eh henga," and at her feet the water of the lagoon lisped along the sand and four downy, young, old-squaw ducklings swam round and round, so quiet, with such bright curious eyes. Okoma slipped a thin sinew thread through the eye of her finest ivory needle and picked up the soft fawnskin. "You," she murmured to the ducklings, "have fine soft suits on already, of black and white small feathers. *My* small duckling must be sewed for. Maybe your mother has plenty to do anyway; here she comes after you now."

She called softly to the worried duck mother. "Ah-ha-lik, ah-ha-lik, you must worry too, must you, just like Inuit mother?"

Okoma laid the straight little garment on the sand. The leg seams and sleeves she had finished, the sleeves sewed up at the ends so the baby could not get his hands out. Now she picked up her stone oolak and carefully cut out an oblong opening between the legs and to the back of this sewed an oblong piece of soft sealskin. Her ivory needle slipped swiftly in and out; the two edges were whipped together evenly and well. Then the sealskin piece must have narrow straps sewed at either corner; thus it could be folded up and tied about the baby's waist, with an extra piece of deerskin inside it for a pad.

As for the top, Okoma sewed from each corner, leaving an opening through which little Enook could be inserted into his new home. Then she must cut out the outer dress, just like this one, only from a lighter piece of deerskin. It was a good thing Toozak had gotten plenty of deerskins from the relatives across the water, last year. And on the front of this second dress she would sew a half circle of white deerskin to hang down under Enook's chin, for her son should have exactly proper clothes; he was the son of Toozak, and grandson of Apangalook, and he must grow to be a great provider. He must have no cold air down his neck, either, so his little mother cut a strap of deerskin to fasten snugly around it. With his fawnskin cap, Enook would be snug and warm, ready to go out in the open air.

Okoma was intent on her fine stitches, but remembered, too, the fire, and the big clay pot of geese. She laid small sticks of wood just the right length on the coals, moved the tripod a bit, peered into the pot. Wonderful good smell of goose; she was getting hungry, and the other hungry people should be coming. She poured in a little more water from the whalebone bucket, and frowned. That crack in the top of the pot was getting wider. Assoonga would have to hurry with the making of new clay pots. She gathered up her precious garments and precious scraps, stuck her bone needles into the tiny strap of deerskin, pulled it up inside a little ivory cylinder and took all into the tent to put away in her oval wooden workbox. As she stepped out again she heard voices. Toozak was coming up the beach, shouting and holding out to her a big gray something. "Look! Feel of this. What do you think?"

Okoma reached her hands quickly for that gray lump. "I think Assoonga will be happy; and here she comes. Hurry, Assoonga, your son has brought some of the good clay."

Assoonga, puffing a bit, put down her loaded poke and knelt before the big brick of clay Okoma laid before her on the sand. Solemnly she rolled bits of it between thumb and finger, squeezed and patted. Her round face became eager and glad. "Ah-ha, this is the kind of clay a woman needs. The clay at the lagoon is always best. I see, Okoma, you have kept the old pot together over the fire today so all hungry ones may eat tonight. Tomorrow we make new pots and the old one can crack wide open if he wishes to."

Toozak stood watching his mother's happy face. Just so must that first mother have looked, for the story went that right here, in this very place, those first people had found clay for their dishes.

CHAPTER XXII

The Best Spirit World

TOOZAK bent and struggled with the stubborn rock. Apangalook pulled on the walrus rope lashing and tried to tighten it. The storm was blowing so hard that the two strong men were blown against the house and must crouch and cling while they got one more heavy weight against the timbers of the passageway. The world was one roar of wind and breakers and pounding rain.

Apangalook grunted, and, holding to a timber, looked along the stout wall of the passageway. "I think it will hold now, but the south wind is not through with us yet. I wonder how a man might build a house to meet the wind any better."

Toozak looked critically up at the house wall, shielding his face from flying sand. "Perhaps in the old land across the water and in other places the wind does not blow as it does on Sevuokuk," he laughed. He glanced up and down the village. "Wohtillin is out fixing his wall, too."

"Yes, and Iyakatan is in there. Old Kotwowin must be lying on the skins again." Toozak, the laughing one, had a very serious face for this moment. Then he followed his father through the small square door, into the passage, into warmth, and relief from the wind's awful strength.

"A sad day for old Kotwowin," thought Toozak. "The wind will sing to her with the voices of all the spirits, calling for her soul."

He paused; Apangalook was stooping in front of him, lifting the heavy deerskin curtain to crawl into the warm house, but Toozak turned and crawled out into the storm again. He couldn't help wanting to know what was going on in the village; just now he wanted to know what was going on in Wohtillin's house.

A small figure came staggering through the roar of blown snow; Wohtil-

163

lin's fat little Tongyan, coming in from his mouse snares. Toozak put his arm about Tongyan's shoulders. It seemed to take a long time to push through flying snow and sand to Wohtillin's door.

The family were all there, and it was warm. Toozak and Tongyan crept over to Tongyan's sleeping place and squatted there, gradually wriggling themselves out of their murre-skin parkas. No one spoke. They looked toward the other end of the house.

There lay good old Kotwowin, Yokho's friend, mother of Wohtillin, in her worn deerskin robe, gray of face and shivering in the hot air of the house. Wohtillin sat by her side. His wife, Rohltungu, was trimming the moss wick of the lamp—the flame grew brighter, the place was growing warmer and warmer. Naked but for breach skin or kalevak, everyone shone with warmth, and still poor Kotwowin shivered and gazed upward with pain in her eyes. Toozak was not sure whether he should have come or not. Though married and already a father, he was still very young, and he had never seen the spirits of death hovering as close as this. He felt fat little Tongyan pressing close to him. Tongyan must have the same cold weight inside him.

At Kotwowin's feet knelt Iyakatan, the old Singer, not Massiu, the young one. Almost as old as Kotwowin, Iyakatan was, but as strong and clever with brews and medicines and charms and singing as Massiu was. By a secret process handed down from the first people of the Island, he had made for Kotwowin some of the good medicine from burned deer antler.

Kotwowin only lay and shivered. She tried to smile when Tongyan crawled near her with bewilderment on his round cheeks, but her poor old teeth chattered together, then, and she could only moan and lay her thin trembling hand on his arm.

Iyakatan held charms in his hands, a seagull skull in one, a crane's bill in the other, and these he shook above his head and all about in the air as he sang the plea to the departed soul to return. His eyes were closed, his thin face stern and sad with the years, and his voice came high and strange as though from far away in the world of spirits. Tongyan returned to his corner and he and Toozak huddled there, gazing, half unwillingly but in an irresistible trance of curiosity. Wohtillin and Rohltungu both sat with bowed heads, but Toozak, in spite of the cold, heavy feeling inside him, must watch. His curiosity, his quick-seeing eye, could not be still.

Iyakatan's voice ceased for a moment. Immediately the voices of the storm penetrated the house—howling and whooping of a furious wind, the slap of gravel blown against the driftwood wall, the never-ceasing roar of the great breakers on the west beach.

Suddenly, Toozak saw that old Kotwowin no longer shivered. She lay quietly, wide-eyed as though listening, and raised her hand to silence the Singer. "Wohtillin, my son."

Wohtillin bent over her. There was no sound but the voice of the storm. Kotwowin looked long into Wohtillin's strong face. "I think the storm will soon die," she said. "But the time of frost under the roof is soon here and your mother cannot live to hear the auklets coming back to the mountain again. This I know. I have a good family here. My spirit will not come back to bring misfortune. When the storm dies, it will be time for me to go, and I should like to go to the best spirit world."

Kotwowin looked all around the room, into the solemn faces of the young boys, the serious wondering eyes of her older grandson, Kulukhon, the tear-filled eyes of her good daughter-in-law, and finally she turned to Iyakatan. "Iyakatan, we have seen many seasons pass over this island, you and I. You have been a good friend. But now you need sing no more."

Kotwowin closed her eyes. They knew she would not open them again in this world although her breathing was light and easy. Iyakatan's hands, with the charms in them, fell to his side. He looked at Wohtillin, and bowed his head, and suddenly, they all realized it was very still. The storm was dying.

Kotwowin had made her choice. She had said she wanted to go to the best spirit world. There was no mistaking what she meant. Toozak had heard his father speak of this thing. Wohtillin rose and put on his parka. Rohltungu brought his boots. There was nothing to be said. Rohltungu sat down in the corner with the two young boys, and bowed her head. Wohtillin picked up his tiny old mother gently; Toozak and Iyakatan lifted the curtain for him and he walked out with his load.

Behind the houses of the village was a long natural depression in the gravel. Toozak, sitting in the house with the silent people, could see in his closed eyes Wohtillin, going down into this place, with Kotwowin on his shoulder. He would be laying her on the ground and she would lie there quietly. Wohtillin would be quickly slipping a noose of mukluk thong over her head, quickly tightening it.

The time seemed long in the house. The storm was tired too; it was only whispering around the walls now. Then they heard a sound in the passage. Iyakatan raised the curtain and Wohtillin entered, carrying the body of

Kotwowin. Behind him Toozak saw Apangalook, and Assoonga, come to help.

Assoonga knew about such matters, just as she knew about bringing people *into* the world. She slipped out of her parka and set to work, Rohltungu bringing things to her as she needed them. There were very few words. Assoonga washed Kotwowin from the soles of her feet to the crown of her head with water, using a towel of twisted grass, then with old seal oil which Rohltungu brought in a little wooden dish.

She now lifted Kotwowin's clothes and turned each piece wrong side out, and with these, Kotwowin was clothed again. Now Wohtillin and Apangalook lifted Kotwowin around so that her feet were on the wooden pillow-log, and laid over her a deerskin with the hair outside.

Toozak went out with his brother-in-law, Kulukhon, and helped to bring in the great platter, with a piece of boiled walrus on it. Rohltungu cut the meat up properly and set the platter on top of the skin covering the dead Kotwowin. All those present sat beside the platter and ate. It was very quiet in the house, with only the sounds of eating. Toozak somehow found it hard to swallow his piece of meat. When the meal was over, all began finding their clothes and turning them wrong side out.

When they were all clothed, Rohltungu went out and gathered some of the strong-smelling plants[1] which grew in the gravel all about the house. It was very warm in the house; Toozak watched Rohltungu, and hoped she would hurry. She was making a bundle of some of the plants and some grass, and she tied this around her head, so that the plants hung down over her face, beside her nose. Wohtillin and Kulukhon did the same, for they were the nearest relatives, and Assoonga stooped over the body and tied some of the plant to it, also.

Now the men were wrapping the body in the deerskin, with a slender stick placed along its length so it could not bend, the whole lashed round with four strips of walrus rope. Rohltungu was rolling into one rain parka all Kotwowin's clothes and the dishes from which she had eaten. This bundle, Iyakatan, being the oldest, carried out on his back.

Outside the house stood Apangalook and two others, Pungwi and Irrigoo. Wohtillin motioned Toozak to stand with them, and he found himself holding one of the four ends of walrus rope. So he was to help old Kotwowin to the mountain she had loved so well! Many, many pokes of nunivak had Kotwowin gathered off its slopes. Toozak could see her now, toiling slowly upward, stooping here and there for the greens, chattering away to the children who were always following her.

The family walked slowly behind the pallbearers, around the house and out across the spit toward the mountain. Halfway across, the men lay down their burden and stood back silently.

Wohtillin and Rohltungu and Kulukhon must do their part. Iyakatan laid down his bundle. Each of the relatives cut a piece of grass from the dry, frozen clumps nearby, and tied these to the body. Then, very thoroughly, they tore to pieces all the clothing in the bundle and dropped them there, and all the dishes they broke with rocks and threw them down. Rohltungu held in her hand for a moment the small, wooden bowl of a reddish color well-darkened by oil, which Kotowwin had had as long as she could remember her. She laid the bowl on the ground at her feet, lifted a good-sized rock, and closed her eyes as she dropped it upon the bowl. The men moved on toward the mountain. Rohltungu walked slowly back toward the house.

Kotwowin was a woman. She would not have to be carried more than half way up the mountain. Toozak looked up toward the top, where the whale-boat captains were buried with their steering paddles pointing south. He had often seen these places, where all the men, still talked of among the people as great hunters in the days gone by, had been laid in the high rocks in great honor. Perhaps some day he, Toozak, could be taken to the top, and his soul fly to a fine country in the sky. At least, there would be the skull of Nanook on his grave.

Now they had found a good rock for shelter. Kotwowin's bearers laid her with head to the north. Iyakatan and the other men took out their knives; a new kind of knife they had now, from their relatives across the water, with a thin but very strong blade. The ropes, the deerskin wrapping, were all cut into pieces and thrown behind the rocks; then Kotwowin's clothing was cut off her in pieces, the pieces thrown away; the stick was laid beside her.

There was nothing more to be done here, and no one wanted to stay long in this place. The sun had gone behind racing dark clouds and the wind still burst at them from the crevices as they walked around the naked body in the direction the sun travels, and started down the mountain side in single file, Iyakatan leading the way.

Iyakatan did not go straight down the mountain. He often stepped aside, and jumped over stones, and sometimes walked backward a few steps, and once he stopped and with a handful of dry plants, brushed himself off all over. Every one of these things the rest must do, too, and Toozak watched carefully, for this was his first funeral experience. Any evil spirits hovering about Kotwowin's grave must be thrown off the trail and brushed away so that they could not follow them into the village. They did not fear for Kotwowin herself; her soul would be going to the best spirit world, up in the sky, though always dragging the mukluk rope with which she had been choked to death. Going thus by her own wish she had made this sure. Wise old Kotwowin; she knew that if she lingered on and died of illness she must go to a sad world where snow would always be blowing in and rain falling from the sky. Toozak felt now that Kotwowin had known best. The cold heavy feeling inside him was not so bad now.

When they had finished their jumping, zig-zag march, and stood before Wohtillin's house again, Rohltungu came out with a fire burning in a clay dish. She set it on the ground in the midst of them and fed the fire with dry sticks and grass, and into it, she and Wohtillin and Kulukhon threw the plants from off their faces. Each man stood over the fire twisting and turning himself to get any harmful spirits or sickness smoked off.

Now Wohtillin gave to each bearer a short piece of mukluk rope cut from the same coil which had lashed the body, and to each an ivory bead strung on a piece of sinew. Silently, Iyakatan and the rest tied the beads to their belts, took the ropes in their hands and walked away, each to his own boat rack where he must tie the piece of funeral rope. The funeral was over but there were still things for them to do. Toozak walked with his father through the cold dusk to the shore. Apangalook would know what to do next.

The storm was dying away into the darkness, but the breakers were still rolling in; they were like armies of ghosts, moving, grasping at the shore with outstretched arms, but never able to hold it, slipping back into blackness again. Toozak stood and watched them a moment and shivered and stooped quickly beside Apangalook to gather some seaweed from the long row thrown up by the storm. Gladly he turned back toward the houses. He was glad that the rest of the necessary things could be done inside where there was warmth. Tomorrow he would receive from Yokho his tattoo spot on each joint for the first funeral he had helped with.

In the house Assoonga pulled off their boots and parkas for them and brought a large bowl of water. Father and son knelt, and, using the grass insole of a boot, washed themselves well. Now they must have a fire in the passageway and into this Assoonga put the seaweed they had brought in. Thick and suffocating the smoke rose, but they must crouch there and hold the clothes they had worn on the mountain over it. Toozak shivered but

Apangalook kept turning his clothes this way and that. "You understand, of course, that you must do this well, else the foxes and seals and all the other animals will smell some dead spirits on us and be scared away from Sevuokuk?"

"Yes, I understand, and it is true also, is it not, that in these next four days when Wohtillin and his family must stay in the agra, that we neighbors cannot do any work in our houses in the evening?"

"Yes, that is the way it is," answered Apangalook. He set the smoking bowl outside and they both crawled quickly into the warm house where Okoma and Assoonga and the rest sat waiting for them. Only Kulukhon was not there; he must stay in his father's house. Apangalook settled himself on his sleeping place, sighed deeply, picked up a piece of baleen he had been stripping for harpoon binding. "The reason for that rule was told by the old people, long ago. They told that if neighbors did work in their houses at night after the burial, the body of the dead would be brought back, wrapped as for its journey to the mountain."

Okoma looked up quickly from her work, and Toozak found he could still smile. He had been away—it seemed far away—for many hours. It was good to get back to Okoma, who still had smiling eyes for him. He leaned close to her and whispered, "You had best put the mitts away; it will soon be dark outside."

Apangalook went on, "They used to tell how this law came to be. There was once a neighbor woman sewing late in the evening after a funeral. Everyone else in her family was asleep. She heard a noise outside as of something being pulled. She kept on sewing and the sound came near. All at once she heard a loud sound beside the house. She jumped up, lit a torch from the lamp, and went out to see what it was."

Sekwo lay at her father's feet, her eyes very round. Apangalook paused. He prided himself that he knew how to tell a story well.

"There, just outside the house, lay a dead body wrapped in deerskin. The woman was so scared she fell dead by the side of it. The next morning the people took both up to the mountain."

. . . . .

Over in Wohtillin's house the family lay in their sleeping places. This had been a hard day, but they had done all as best they knew and sleep was coming. For four more days they would stay in here, never putting their heads out unless they had their hoods up and an eye shade on, for during these days, Kotwowin's soul might still be wandering about, not quite ready to start away on its long journey, and it was not good for any of her people to come in contact with it.

Early on the fifth morning, Wohtillin would lead them to the grave, and, returning, they would walk backward a good part of the way to the house. Then they could turn their clothes right side out again and go about, if they kept their hoods up, but they could not go to the shore for six days, till all scent of death was faded from them. When the ten days had passed and all the dishes they had been eating from had been broken and thrown away, the ceremonies would all be ended and life would go on.

Rohltungu thought of all these things as she lay there that first night. The wind had gone far away and it was very still. Now a restless dog outside howled a long, low note. Another long howl answered him from the other end of the village. Howling of dogs was the usual background of nights on Sevuokuk, but tonight they sounded different. Rohltungu lay and listened and was sad. Old Kotwowin's place near the door was dark and empty. Perhaps the dogs would be going to the mountain.

CHAPTER XXIII

After the Storm

THE BEACH was the place these days. The big storm had left mountains of interesting things above the tide line, and here the women and children were busy.

"People have turned into snipes this day," laughed Toozak. He and Timkaroo were on their way to the beach to try for tomcod with Timkaroo's new throwing net of finely shredded sinew.

"Yes, look at Sekwo," answered Timkaroo. "She makes a fine snipe; runs fast and stops quickly."

Sekwo was having an exciting time. In her quick movements here and there, poking in the piles of seaweed with a piece of walrus rib, she had already found two big starfish and a whole bed of the slender oily fish Assoonga liked to boil. The storm had brought in so many of them that they were piled one upon another in a long silvery strip between the seaweeds.

"Look, Sekwo," cried Kaka, "here is a long queer one."[1] Kaka, that smiling one, held up a long, slender fish, round like a blown intestine. "Ah-k," laughed Sekwo. "He is no good, but is he not strange to look at? Look at the hole he has on each side. Throw him away; maybe the seagulls will like him."

Sekwo could not remember ever having more fun. She and Kaka and little Notangi slid and slipped along over the rocks but somehow it was always Sekwo and Kaka who traveled together and found the most surprises. Every cranny was piled with gifts of the storm. The little bulbs of the brown seaweed[2] popped beneath their feet; the green seaweed[3] was slimy and slippery to step on with moccasined feet but under every frond they must poke with their pieces of rib. Who could tell what they might find?

Ever since they could remember, these two busy ones had run over the tundra and along the beaches together, hunting, laughing, quarreling together. The cries and chatter of Walla and Assoonga and the other women and the children floated back along the beach, with the voices of the gulls that had not gone south who were so noisy in their search of the wonderful storm shore.

Sekwo caught up to Walla, and held out to her a handful of beautiful, tiny fish with shiny sides. Walla's square, jolly face became sober when she looked at the shiny fish. "Ah, girl, you will have to put those back. They are very fine little fish but we do not eat them. The old people say some harm might befall us if we ate them. But take your piece of rib and poke around in that little pool over there between the rocks. You might find a charm for little Enook."

Walla bent her sturdy back again to pull more of the leafy kind of kelp out from among the rocks; she had quite a pile of it on the sand already. She would have a good many braids of it to dry and store away for winter, and she knew how good it would taste in the cold dark days, boiled with seal or walrus.

As for Sekwo, she left Kaka poking about among the mussels and clams; she had something more important to do. She knelt on a flat rock beside the little pool. The tiny red starfish[4] would be the finest kind of charm for the little nephew, Toozak's son.

Sekwo's smooth face was warm and her brow creased in a worried look as she poked about among the seaweed and tiny eels, white clams and sponges stranded in the tide pool. She picked out a few shrimps and one big six-pointed starfish. Tokoya would cook these for them. She even found four sea cucumbers and laid them in the pile at her side. These were all fine things to eat, but her heart was set on the rare gift which would protect little Enook from all harm.

The water of the pool was now all stirred up. She sat back and waited for it to clear again. Kaka was calling out that he had found a big toopook.[5] Sekwo saw him holding the broad-headed thing up; its skin was transparent and marked in curious ways. She knew Kaka would give it to old Yokho because only the old people could eat toopook. It would stop the growth of young ones. Up on the beach above her she saw that the women had many piles of seaweed ready, each kind in a different pile, Aghnoghook,[6] Opa[7] and many others. Aghnoghook's bulbs were mouse-shaped when open and old Yokho had told Sekwo that if they became ripe enough to open they became live mice, running about on the inland tundra. And Kaka was stringing on a piece of mukluk rope a big collection of pink sculpins. Sekwo sat back on her heels, and watched and wished she had one, with a bowl of seal oil to dip the pieces in; that made a fine meal for anyone.

She bent down over her tide pool again. Oh, generous spirits! There on the opposite side, almost hidden in a little rock crevice under the water's edge, was something red. Sekwo ran and leaned over. Yes! The starfish, red and beautifully shaped! Breathlessly she slipped her hand under it. Sekwo quickly gathered all her treasures into her little sealskin pouch and skipped down over the rocks and among the heaps of seaweed to Walla, then on down to the shore where the men were fishing for cod.

As she ran she saw Timkaroo and Pungwi drop their hooks and lines and run to Toozak. Toozak, laughing more than ever, was standing on a rock a little way out from shore, holding up a big fish, not a codfish. Sekwo reached the water's edge as her brother came splashing recklessly in, the big fish in one hand, in the other, a stick with a loop of baleen at its end. "Ah, Toozak," cried Pungwi, "so you have snared Makeetluk[8] of the sharp teeth?"

Toozak knelt and laid the long fish on the beach at Sekwo's feet. His face was shining. Pungwi lifted the fish's head, opened its jaws; inside were rows of the sharpest teeth Sekwo had ever seen. Pungwi nodded his head and smiled at Sekwo, "When Makeetluk's head is very well dried, your little nephew Enook will wear it hanging on his belt. It is one of the finest charms."

Silently, then, she held up to Pungwi her red starfish. "Ah-k, what is this?" they all cried at once. "A good girl this is. Enook will now have not only one, but two powerful charms. Health and good fortune will surely be his."

Toozak was too happy to fish more today. Okoma had borne him a son, a mighty little hunter, and he and Sekwo had been granted the good fortune of finding two of the best charms for him right away. And he had sometimes thought this round-faced little sister a nuisance! He took her by the hand now and they hurried home to make Okoma happy.

Walla laid down her load of braided seaweed in the outer room. Kaka and little Okohoni were hanging their fish to dry on the meat rack outside; they might freeze before they dried much, but either way, with seal oil to dip each piece in, they would be fine food for the time, until the winter ice came again.

Walla lifted the curtain and slid into the warm house. Pungwi was already there, his catch of codfish was already on the rack. They had all done a good day's work and Walla hurried now to get the lamp going brightly and some fish boiling in the pot hanging over it. She helped Pungwi pull off his clothes; the little place was getting warm and that was a comfort, for the storm was coming back again; no woman could use an outdoor fireplace tonight; the wind was rising again to a cold shriek outside the walls.

Walla, stooping over the lamp, looked over her shoulder at Pungwi. She wondered—it was that time of year, and Pungwi was so quiet tonight, as though his mind was on something else. He, whose round cheeks were nearly always pushed high beside his bright eyes with smiling, was solemn now, and of course she could not say anything to him, for he had not spoken to her yet. But she was pretty sure he was thinking of wapacha.[9]

Yes, in a few minutes she saw him pull down the gutskin sack from the wall. Here were five wapacha, picked in midsummer, pulled apart and dried.

Pungwi looked now at Walla and said, "I think it is time for the good dreaming. Bring me the bowl of water."

Kaka and Okohoni came in. Pungwi was sitting on his sleeping place, putting one piece of wapacha after another into his mouth, taking big swallows of water from the bowl at his side. He did this slowly, looking at each piece, smiling at it, before he put it into his mouth.

Walla and the two boys sat about the meat platter and ate fresh boiled fish, but Pungwi sat on his robe, a quiet listening look on his face. Suddenly he rose, and began walking up and down in the little room. "Now, I am getting lighter—my body has no weight—do you hear? My limbs are as though they were hollow."

Walla gathered up the dishes and set them outside. "Yes, we hear you speak. Wapacha is taking you into the dream already."

She motioned to the two boys to sit quietly, far back in the corner. Their father was pacing faster and faster. At times he stopped as though listening to the wind howling outside. His eyes roved here and there. Walla knew he would be very easily frightened right now; she was glad when he fell suddenly upon his bed and was asleep.

All night and all the next day Pungwi slept, but it was no ordinary sleep; it was a sleep which would frighten anyone who did not understand wapacha. He lay on his back, his lips drawn back, foam bubbling between his teeth and in his nostrils, sweat standing out all over him, his breath long and rasping. Every little while the watchers saw his limbs jerk in every joint, but no sounds came from his lips.

Toward evening, Iyakatan and Apangalook and Toozak came in and sat, watching. Walla had just trimmed the lamp, and in the yellow dusk they all sat quietly; the wind was still blowing, singing in many voices about the house. Pungwi stirred and opened his eyes and looked at Toozak, but Toozak was sure he was not seeing him. He then stared straight into the lamp flame and began rocking back and forth and singing in a loud voice not at all like his own. "He is singing of what he saw in this first dream," murmured Iyakatan, "but he will not sing long; this is only the first waking."

Toozak noticed how calmly Iyakatan spoke. He had had wapacha dreams, too. A Singer must know all these things. As for himself, his head felt as though it would burst soon. He had lived through so much in the past few days. Kotwowin's death, the big storm, the snaring of Makeetluk, and now, this wapacha dream of Pungwi's. Yet, of course, he would not go home. He was curious as always, and this thing Pungwi was doing was strange and new to him. The voice which came from Pungwi's lips, yet was not Pungwi, suddenly ceased. Toozak leaned forward. Pungwi's legs and arms began to jerk and he fell back onto his sleeping robe and slept again.

The friends sat there in the dim warm room, watching Pungwi's joints and even his muscles pulsing and jerking. He was not sweating so much now and there was no foam at mouth or nostrils. Once again he awoke and sat up and sang in such a loud, unceasing kind of voice that they knew he was far away from them—no one could interrupt him; he did not hear.

In a little while the strange voice stopped; Pungwi fell over and slept again. Still his friends sat through the dark hours, and Massiu was there also by this time. Apangalook's head was sunk on his chest and the two young boys were sound asleep on their robes. Walla still sat gazing at her husband, lying there like a naked stranger, arms and fingers and toes moving like separate live souls, and Toozak, the curious one, and Massiu, the thoughtful one, sat and watched with her and saw all.

The wind died to a whisper outside the walls, the lamp was burning with a very low flame; Walla knew it must be another day. Pungwi suddenly opened his eyes and spoke in a weak voice. "Wapacha is going out now."

Walla leaned toward him, "Do you wake up now, Pungwi?"

"Yes, I have been in a big trance. This dream was very good."

Apangalook's head jerked up. The two sleeping boys awoke. Massiu and

Iyakatan both leaned toward Pungwi. In a few minutes he spoke again; "Wapacha is all out now. It is the best kind of dream."

"You were in a very deep trance," said Walla. "We were very much frightened."

"No, no," answered Pungwi, "it was all very good."

He sat up and looked around at all the good faces turned so expectantly toward him, and he smiled at them, his own smile. He pulled his knees up, leaned his arms across them and sat, very weak but very calm. "Now I may tell you of my big journey. I have been on that journey to see my people who died long ago."

When I felt myself getting lighter and lighter I left this house and looking around, saw a man with only one leg and one arm. Another man like him came then, but he had a short beard. The first one asked, "Why do you eat us?"

I told him, "There is somebody always makes me feel bad. I want to see his place."

These two men took me to the place. It was the place where the dead are buried. We then went underground and saw many different places. At one place we found an old man. "This," the cripples said to me, "is the man who makes you feel sad." But I did not know the old man. The cripples then said, "Take off your clothes and give them to this dead man." I said, "I would do this, but look out for my relatives then!"

We left this place and the cripples asked me what place next. "Do you want to see other things?"

I said, "I want to see the destroyers of other people."

We went above the ground and went forth. The ground under us now was going very fast and I saw all kinds of devils.

"Do you wish to see the Creator?" And they went on to take me to see him. It was a very fast trip. When we arrived, the Creator's house was shown to me. I wanted to go in. Going inside we saw a man with pillows under his knees sitting close to the door. When he looked at me he could also turn to look the other way. He said to me, "How did you come here?"

"Wapacha took me here."

"If wapacha took you up, sit down, but only on one cheek." The Creator then called a man in the inner room. We heard a noise inside and while that person came closer, the room was getting colder and colder. I began to get so cold my teeth began to chatter, so that I could hardly speak. I said, "I

don't want to stay here longer. It's so cold. I want to go out."

The Creator on the pillow told me, "I would like to tell you much about our place here but I see you can not stand the cold, so you better go."

The Creator spoke in our language but the big noise spoke in the language of the Chukchee people across in the old land. He said, "Why didn't you come with more clothes? But you must be strong, coming here with only one parka."

I felt I wanted to sing then, but the Creator told me to go out. When I went out it was very cold. With the two cripples I went very fast, coming down. They said, "Do you want to see the burial place again?"

I said, "Yes, I want to see it." So we went into the ground again. It was a very bad place, with so many worms, so much dripping of water from above. But there was some fresh water. If only I had had a cup I could have drunk. From other pools I could have drunk, too, with my head down, but there were too many worms in it. I told them, "Next time I will always take a cup along so I will not die of sickness, so that I will have a chance to hang myself and go above to a better place."

I backed out of that place and we all three walked, but the cripples said, "But you can not go back to earth now. You must stay here for five years."

Then it seemed that I could not stand that place for five years, so it seemed to me that I died there. Just then one of the cripples said, "Just look, your house is very close."

Very quickly I ran to my house, but when I got here five men were here, the five men I had eaten—wapacha. All of a sudden, I took to the air, flying very fast. I came to a cliff, and on the very tallest point I caught my toe, which stopped me. I sat there on the point of the cliff and looked down and I saw large breakers and the five men playing, below. Now I felt my feet slipping all the time and gave up to die again. I kept slipping but caught myself on a little knoll.

One of the wapacha called to me to smile at him just as I had smiled at him when I ate him. Now the five began to look like shadows. But we all started for home again. When I came close to the house one man called to me to look at my house. The house came toward me. It came in two parts. The upper one with the roof came over me and together we flew toward Heaven. One of the voices said, "Now look at your boat rack."

The bow of my boat too flew up and with me. I felt so much surprised. Why did they do it this way? Then I was up there with the Creator and it seemed years went by. Then someone said my son Kaka had sent the other half of my house and boat up to the Creator. The wapacha men went behind the house. The Creator said, "Sacktayah! You can go home now."

Then I flew toward the south like a duck. Very fast. When coming to my house I saw something fastened to it which was nearly broken off. It was a line leading into the house. I thought, "What is this, this line into my house?"

I followed the line into the house, into the inner room, and there I saw myself, lying, belly up, sleeping. Then I woke up, and find that I have never really left or been away.

CHAPTER XXIV

Siko Again

AKOMAK, the month of sitting, was over half gone and Siko had not been sighted. The old men climbed up and looked each morning, just as they had done in that first hunting year that Toozak remembered so well. And over at Kukulik on the other side of the island, they knew the old men there must be on the big cliff every day, pounding with a well-worn, round stone on their big pounding rock, calling for the north wind with all their strength.

Then Siko came, quickly, and strongly, attached itself to the shore ice in great fields until all the world was white again. And with Siko, of course, there were Iviek and Noghsuk and Mukluk and all the rest, and the hunters were out early and late. The women were kept busy repairing clothing and drying it each night, inspecting every boot, every bit of clothing, for the tiniest hole or loosening in the seam.

. . . . .

It was only mid-day but most of the hunters had gone ashore to put their meat away. Three of the youngest, Timkaroo, Toozak and Kulukhon, and three of the older hunters, Pungwi, Ikmallowa and Iyakatan, were still out on the ice. Iyakatan had found a small open place and already they had killed two walrus in it and were hurrying with the cutting up, for it was a long drag to shore for so much meat and blubber.

Iyakatan had remembered, when they had harpooned the second walrus, to throw a tuft of fur from his polar bear hunting pants into the water of the hole; he had been glad to see the current was still north. Since he and Ikmallowa, the oldest men, were on the ice themselves today, there was no one watching from the shore.

179

Toozak and Timkaroo tugged at the stomach of the last walrus as Iyaka-tan cut it out of the body. The walrus was a young male; tender mangona that would be. "No time for clam feast today, I guess," laughed Timkaroo. "Too much meat to drag ashore before dark. This breathing hole should have been a little closer in, but it was a good one."

He straightened from his cutting and looked toward the village; hours of tramping back and forth, before they could crawl into warm houses—but where *was* the village? "Ah-ee, ah-ee," screamed Timkaroo, "Iyakatan, Ikmallowa, look, we are moving; south current has come."

Timkaroo ran. They all ran. Like foxes before the dogs they ran, over the rough ice, leaping and jumping, toward the solid shore ice. Too late. A strip of open water lay there, between them and the shore ice, and, for this one time, there were no watchers on the beach. They had all taken their walrus heads inside the houses for the ceremonies.

The six hunters stood and looked at their homes, slipping out of their sight as the current which ran down Sevuokuk's shores like a mighty river carried them southwestward too fast. Too fast, too far.

Iyakatan watched the strip of water, and the shore ice. Other floes would soon close in again so that a boat could not get out from shore, even if there had been someone to see what was happening, and the floe they were on—he turned and looked—it stretched far to the westward; it was a big one, but all being carried swiftly south and west.

Suddenly Iyakatan remembered that he must speak, must say something. No one could speak in this crisis until he, the oldest one, spoke. "The spirits have forgotten six Inuit today it would seem," he said in a soft voice. "But if we use the knowledge passed down from our fathers we may live to hear again the soft laughter of children in the houses when the lamps are burning brightly."

Toozak, the laughing one, he who was always making fun, fell to his knees on the ice and buried his face in his big dogskin mitts. Only last night he had lain on the furs in the warm house playing the game of ivory ducks with Sekwo, while the fortunate baby with all his charms, gurgled and choked at Okoma's breast.

Kulukhon and Timkaroo kept looking toward the shore, and Toozak had to look, too. Cold fear, like squirming eels of the tide pools, crawled through his belly. The hunting beach, several miles below the village, was slipping past now, the big snow-covered cliffs, the bird catching place coming into sight. Toozak remembered the eggs and birds he had gathered over there on those cliffs, suspended in midair by a walrus rope, in the moon of Penahvek, in a world of shining grass and blue flowers and bird songs and thundering surf. Could it all be so changed? Was this thing really happening to him?

Iyakatan moved. "We must go back to the meat. That is our life. We must drag it further away from the breathing hole, for the ice may be weak at that place."

Iyakatan and Ikmallowa knew what they must do. Before the night was altogether black they had one walrus skinned out. It was hard work to do in a hurry and took all their thoughts and all their strength. The three young tugged at the other meat, dragging it back from the hole. Darkness shut the island from view, perhaps forever. The blur of whiteness all around them met the blackness of night and there were no stars. The wind picked up loose snow and ice crystals and rasped them over the floe and flung them into the hunters' faces, but it was not blowing as they knew it could blow. They heard no grinding of ice. Iyakatan thought they were still moving, but so quietly there was no sound but the wind.

Pungwi piled the last of the blubber scrapings from the hide at one side and stepped into the hide, tramping about on it. In a few days it would shrink and pull up around the edges and they would have a shallow bowl to sit and sleep in; so much better than lying on the ice. The six of them sat there now, close together, and ate the clams from one walrus stomach. The clams were still a little warm, and very comforting. Toozak licked the juice from his fingers. "Ah-ee, perhaps we shall be back in front of the village when morning comes and a change of tide," he murmured drowsily to Timkaroo, and curled up in a ball. Young people must sleep no matter what comes.

"Hi, hi, Toozak," Iyakatan reached over and shook him. "You are not ready to sleep yet; look you here, and do as I show you if you would live to see your family again."

Iyakatan pulled off his fur boots; fine ice boots they were, with thick soles of young walrus hide. Iyakatan tucked the boots up under his reindeer parka after he had pulled out the grass insoles, then pulled off his fawnskin socks, too. The socks he placed inside his outer parka, one sock on each shoulder. Now he pushed back his parka hood, put the grass insoles on top of his head, and put the hood on again. Toozak was following his motions, as were the others, but he gazed at his bare feet, and then at Iyakatan's. What about them? Iyakatan smiled, "Better to have your feet a little cold at night than to have them swell inside your boots and become dead flesh."

He reached behind him for his hunting bag, took out some of the harpoon heads, sharpening stone and other things and laid them aside. Out of the bag then came the extra pair of dogskin mitts every hunter carries. All the others pulled mitts from their bags, too, watching Iyakatan. He looked around the circle. "Good—if we do not freeze, we shall thank the clever women who examined all our gear last night. Put your bare feet into the extra mitts, pull the hunting bag over both."

Iyakatan pulled his outer pants of polar bear fur down a bit over his knees, curled up, and lay still. Close beside him lay Toozak, then the other four, ready for sleep, with the dog fur on their parka hoods pulled well over their faces.

. . . . .

Iyakatan was a stern master but they never questioned his wisdom. They had slept twelve sleeps on the ice and were still alive, still drifting about on an endless white field shrouded most of the time in fog and dusk and darkness, for these were the short days and the sun never could climb over the low hanging banks of cloud and fog and winter mist. They knew they must be shifting back and forth with every change of the tide, and their world was full of horrible noises of grinding and crashing and groaning at times, so that they all expected the ice to part beneath their feet, but the main south current still held them and carried them gradually farther and farther away from the island, and still their own floe remained whole.

Each morning they must walk. Around and around the heap of walrus meat and skins and bones which was their home, they went, but never very far, and never very far from one another. They all knew the ice could break and split; it was not necessary to speak of that.

Toozak followed Iyakatan's orders like a child; it seemed to him that he had always lived like this—tramping round and round on this whiteness with grayness hanging over his shoulders; perhaps he had only dreamed that he was Toozak of Sevuokuk, the joker, the happy young father of a lucky son. Lucky! How could he be now, with no father?

Then Iyakatan would say, "Enough of that for today; we must not wear our bootsoles out."

And they would go back to the walrus hide and sit or lie there.

One day, when the fog lifted for a little while, they could see some strange land in the west. Their own they had lost very soon, and this, they saw, was not even the familiar peaks of that part of the old land they had seen all their lives, across the ice or across the water, but some altogether strange looking country, and as the world of ice moved and circled, froze solid, and moved again with awful sounds, they sometimes saw this new land rather plainly, then again it was hidden or far away. They knew their only hope of life was to reach that land someday before starvation or drowning took them.

They lived on, quietly following Iyakatan's words and Ikmallowa's calm example, day by day through this dream. Toozak sometimes sat looking eastward with tears rolling down his cheeks; but nothing was said. Toozak was still very young.

When it was too bitter cold and they could not bear the frozen raw walrus longer, Pungwi would shave a few more tiny shavings off his harpoon shaft and take his fire-making kit from his hunting bag, and they would burn blubber and roast some meat on the tip of a spear, and cheer themselves with the wonderful heat. Then, while they were still a little bit warm, they would crawl onto the hide and pull the other hide up over them and soon it would be almost good in there, and they would try to forget the ache of homesickness and the heavy feeling of death inside them, and Ikmallowa and Iyakatan would tell all the stories their fathers had told to them, and these were many and took hours to tell; so the time passed.

One day, Kulukhon saw a black thing far across the ice and he and Timkaroo ventured over there, and found a walrus in a very small breathing hole. Timkaroo harpooned it and Kulukhon lanced it; then there was work for everybody that day. To be cutting up fresh meat and sweating and grunting with labor again, that was a wonderful relief. And a great thing, to have plenty of meat and another skin, too. Toozak let himself think the spirits might mean to release them from death after all.

But the next day was not so good. Iyakatan and Ikmallowa lay on the hide and could not get up. Their faces were gray and their eyes were bright. "One of my years should have known better than this," moaned Iyakatan. "Ikmallowa and I have eaten too much of the liver and kidneys. It is best that you, Pungwi, take what is left of them and bury it far over where the three young ones will not find them. This walrus must have been one of the flesh-eating kind, and their organs are poison to Inuit."

Pungwi's face was less round and smiling now. He untied the mukluk rope belt from around his waist and pulled from under his parka the neck part of a walrus stomach in which he carried snow next his own stomach to melt into drinking water. He untied the sinew at one end and anxiously poured some water into the sick men's mouths. There was very little one could do—no way of boiling meat into healing broth.

Days were gray and nights were black; only once in a while the clouds lifted and stars were large and close and made the lost souls hope again. At least they were something to look at and think about, and the Dipper and the Arrow were like friends to see again and they knew by them they were drifting south and west.

But pain and misery lived with the two kind old men and would not move. It is hard for a Singer to heal himself. Sometimes in the long starlit hours of a clear night Iyakatan's song wavered out, oh so weakly, over the stillness, waking no echoes—heard only by five sad souls there on the ice. How could it reach to his wandering soul or to Ikmallowa's—to the stars?

But Iyakatan and Ikmallowa knew there was yet a way.

Finally, there came a clear night of bright moonlight when even the hills of that strange land could be seen, but far away, when Iyakatan and Ikmallowa had lain on the walrus hide for fourteen sleeps, when for three sleeps they had lain there too weak to speak. Toozak sat cross-legged looking up at the moon. He lived in memories now. Tonight he remembered old Kotwowin, who had told him about the moon when he was a small boy. The moon was a man with a pail in his hand, and little boys like Toozak must not look at him, for he might throw his pail at them and that would offend the spirits, for the pail belonged to some of them. Toozak drew down his mouth and grimaced at the moon. It would seem sure that the spirits were so much offended now that nothing they did would change things. He could look at the moon all he wished. Beside him Iyakatan

stirred. "Ikmallowa, are you ready? It is as well to go now as any time; I think we have strength for only one more thing."

Iyakatan and Ikmallowa sat up and raised themselves on trembling knees and each pulled out from his belt a new fine-edged hunting knife. Toozak looked at his grandfather and then hid his face in his arms, and Pungwi spoke in a choked voice, "Are you sure you must do this thing?"

Ikmallowa's furrowed face was calm. "Iyakatan has spoken and his word I am ready to follow; my strength is gone. If you live to see our people again, tell them how Iyakatan the Singer and Ikmallowa the hunter went honorably to the happy world of spirits in the sky."

He laid a hand for a moment on Toozak's bowed head, then raised his parka. The knife tip was very cold. It would have to be a strong thrust.

. . . . .

There was a small hummock of jumbled snow and ice not far from their camp on the floe. In this were Iyakatan and Ikmallowa buried.

CHAPTER XXV

With the South Wind

THAT SAD WINTER dragged away at last on Sevuokuk, and summer came, and still another winter. Long, long months.

Gay Toozak, who had kept the whole village laughing through all these years, was gone, and the five others. There could be no doubt now, and Okoma looked very different, without her smile, and Tokoya and Ega no longer had the bright color of tundra flowers in their cheeks. Those three, the happiest young wives on the island, were now sad young widows living as in a dark dream the long winter days. They did not lack for food or skins; Apangalook and Assoonga gave them all this, but they could not give them gladness, out of their own sad hearts, and in the house of Apangalook the long dark days were very different than they had ever been before.

Even so, the second spring came in time—the south wind had cleaned the mountainside of snows, the first baby walrus had been brought in long before, and the young people's voices rang up and down the beaches in the evenings. Wohtillin and his crew brought in a whale, and the birds had come back.

Kaka and Okohoni and Tongyan climbed up through the big boulders and crossed the top of the mountain, jumping from one big rock to another. They carried all sorts of things. Kaka and Okohoni each had a sinew bird net thrown over his hunting bag on his back, and each carried a light slender pole across his back, under his arms, his chest out, just as Toozak had always done. It was the proper way to travel.

Tongyan and Kaka carried some short sticks, too, and in Okohoni's two hands he also carried a big chunk of mud. Okohoni was a bit clumsy. He was dressed in girl's clothes and the boots were uncomfortable. He had been sick and of course Walla felt she must disguise him so that the evil spirits

187

could not recognize him.

Not far from the edge of the cliff, where the birds were skimming in and out in clouds, Kaka began showing the younger ones how to build a bird trap. "Look, here we will build the two pillars; bring flat rocks."

In a few moments there were two rock pillars, with a stout mukluk rope strung between them. From this rope hung many short thin strips of baleen, fluttering in the breeze. Kaka had carried all this rope with strips already tied on, rolled up in his bag.

"Now we find a place to hide," he said. Okohoni and Tongyan slid down behind Kaka into a niche in the rocks. Here they fitted the nets to the long sticks, held them motionless before them on the rocks, and waited. Three tufted puffins[1] came whirring along close overhead, but Kaka did not move. "We do not want them—old women—they do not taste good."

"Why do you say 'old women'?" asked Okohoni, down in the very bottom of the crevice, untangling a skein of baleen.

"Because they *were*," answered Kaka. He made a swoop at a crested auklet[2] but missed it—the breeze was pretty strong, and sat down again. It was cozy down there in the rocks, out of the wind. Kaka talked very softly, so no bird would know there were boys around.

"You all know that whenever our people go camping, they are not allowed to have fires in the open air after the sun goes down for fear the evil spirits will come. One summer, some people went to get birds at the cliffs far to the south of our village. Among them were two women who lived together in a small topek.

"One evening, these women built a fire in the open air in front of their topek. The neighbors tried to stop them from cooking so late in the evening but they did not pay attention to them. They made their fire blaze high and sat beside it. It grew darker but still they were cooking. While they were cooking, a neighbor saw a huge flame of fire appear on the horizon. The neighbor came to the women and told them to quench the fire but they let it burn.

"The pillar of fire came nearer and nearer and when it came so close these two women hit their lips with their hands, hard, and jumped into the fire, and came up out in the water. Their forms were changed to that of puffins. The long feather tuft that is behind their heads was the braided hair. So the puffins were once women."

Kaka stopped short and sprang up behind Tongyan who was aiming his net into the middle of a thick flock of auklets. "Ah-ee," cried Tongyan.

Kaka sprang to help. Each net held a little black and white struggling bird. They were not to cease struggling, yet. Tongyan and Kaka each carried one to the rope between the pillars, pushed the tip of a baleen strip through its nostrils and tied it. There hung the auklets, alive and frantic, fluttering their dark wings as fast as they could.

Kaka and his helpers crept back into their hole and watched. Yes, here were three more, come to find out what had happened to their brothers, fluttering and swooping around the captives. Tongyan and Kaka caught them and added them to the line.

When the mukluk line was nearly full, when the first auklets caught had fluttered themselves to death and been replaced by new live ones, Kaka aimed a quick stroke of his net at a glistening black bird which bolted in over the cliff top. He beckoned to Okohoni, "Now you can try for your cormorants."

He bit the bird quickly in the back of its neck and handed the dead body to Okohoni. Okohoni brought his lump of mud and his sticks and set to work. On the edge of the cliff, on just such a rock as comorants always chose, he set the dead one, plastered the mud all over and about his feet to hold them steady, propped a stick up with one end at the back of the bird's head. There sat the cormorant, 'Ngelkuk,' as true as life, and Okohoni crept back into the crevice to wait for those sociable ones to come to roost near their friend, and so be caught in Kaka's quick net.

Good netting and snaring this day. The birds were still arriving from the south and swirled in crying, noisy clouds across the face of the cliff. Kaka knelt and leaned over; every rock ledge and pillar had birds on it, it seemed. Far below were some columns standing out from the cliff and there sat cormorants, on every little space. Kaka wished they would come up. Okohoni and Tongyan came and lay there, too, looking over.

The breeze was freshening; the sun sometimes broke through the mist and lit the surf below into shining foam breaking and sucking at the feet of the broken pillars.

"Last summer when we went to see my father's people in Kukulik," said Kaka, "I saw the three great rocks, and the ropes hanging on them where Kukulik people go to get young birds and eggs."

"Are the rocks on the shore?" asked Okohoni.

"No, they stand up far from shore, out in the waves. The people over there tell that once there was one of their women who was very angry over something. She went to the high shore across from the place where the rocks are now, and kicked at the rocks of the cliff. She kicked so hard that the cliff fell, far out into the water, and made the three tall rocks."

"They say that the Kukulik people save the bones of all the birds they take from these rocks, and take them back to the place the next time they go there. They are afraid that if they do not do this the birds will leave the rocks. And every summer they put up new walrus hide ropes, so they can climb up to the nests."

Kaka dove at a cormorant with his bolas, but Ngelkuk was swift. Kaka lay down again beside Tongyan. "Are the birds on these rocks you tell about the same as our birds here?"

"Yes, but there are two very small birds there, too, no bigger than the snow bunting, and the people say these are the spirits that own the rocks; that they have changed their forms to birds."

Okohoni saw some murres coming, and sprang back to the hiding place. He was a small boy, but with both hands he swung the net and caught a murre as neatly as could be. No one was more surprised than Okohoni. "Oh-ho," laughed Kaka, "so you are becoming a bird netter already! Come, do not stand there as though frozen and stare. Kill your bird!"

But Okohoni was not staring at the bird—he was staring at Tongyan. Tongyan had a queer look. He was leaning over the top of the rock and gazing out over the water as one who could not move his eyes.

"There," pointed Kaka suddenly, "is that where you are looking, Tongyan?"

Now they all saw. A black spot far far out to westward; a black spot which never went under water, but stayed up, sometimes out of sight behind a wave, then up again. "Ungiak!" cried Kaka. "Let us get down!"

Tongyan suddenly began stuffing birds into his bag. They were all scrambling now. Okohoni forgot his uncomfortable girl's boots and down the mountain they went. Just as Tokoya and Ega had done on that other bright summer day, they raced down the slopes and into the village.

. . . . .

The women were gathered at Wohtillin's house. It was such a mild day that they sat on the ground just outside the doorway. Walla and Assoonga and Anatoonga were busy chewing mukluk hides cut out for boot soles. Okoma came and sat with them, the fat-cheeked little Enook riding on her neck, his face bobbing up and down over her head. Okoma held his two feet in her hands; nearly three years old he was, but he would still ride on his mother's neck, still get his food from her breast, for a long time yet. Anatoonga looked at her daughter. She was still the finest looking woman in the village, sad-eyed as she was.

Rohltungu and wrinkled old Yokho were inside the doorway, both bent double over a little wooden bowl. Finally Yokho was satisfied; soot from the lamp wick and urine had been mixed in proper proportions. "Yokho must have everything just right," murmured Walla to Tokoya.

"Umm-mm," answered Tokoya, her teeth busy with the mukluk skin; she was just turning the sole and it took all her attention. "The color is not so good if things are not mixed just right," went on Walla, the sociable one. "Yokho learned from Kotwowin, and Kotwowin knew a very great deal about tattooing. She made us all seemly looking when we were young girls and the color has stayed, too."

Walla looked, perhaps a bit proudly, at her own hands. She had the most elaborate design of any woman in the village, and her face was fully decorated, too.

Yokho set her little bowl on a whale-vertebra stool inside the doorway, where she could have good light but be protected from the breeze, and Assoonga called in a soft voice, "Come now, Sekwo, Yokho is ready."

Sekwo came slowly but without a word. This was going to hurt, but murmuring about it would do no good. She was twelve years old now and she knew she must be tattooed, or else, when she grew a little older, the other girls in the village would talk scornfully of her behind her back, as one who had not the courage to become beautiful and desirable.

Yokho was kind. She smiled at her favorite granddaughter and sat her down on another stool, and Rohltungu held the child's head steady in her two hands.

Yokho picked up her fine ivory needle fastened into a little wooden handle, dipped it in the bowl, thrust it into Sekwo's cheek at the top of her cheek bone. Three times she thrust the needle in, then dipped her finger in the soot and rubbed it briskly over the pricks; they showed a fine deep blue. Sekwo's eyes filled with tears, but her teeth were clenched and she made no sound.

"Ah-ha," murmured Rohltungu, turning Sekwo's head to the other side. "That is a fine beginning for your tattoo. Fine smooth skin the girl has; she will take a beautiful tattoo, will she not, Yokho?"

"Yes, it is a good beginning," answered Yokho, "she is brave enough. She will never have to be like Ingangowin of Kukulik."

"Ah-h," agreed all the women, and Assoonga smiled a proud little smile at her daughter. She knew about Ingangowin of Kukulik. She was the weak one who had refused to be tattooed, until of course she had to have some tattoo when her first child was born. Still she refused to have the full tattoo, until misfortunes, one after another drove her to it—sickness, and the death of two children. Then at last she had the full tattoo to try to change her appearance and mislead the harmful spirits. Poor Ingangowin, if she had only followed the old women's words in the first place!

Now Sekwo had six pricks on each cheek, and one cheek was already swelling a bit. Rohltungu rubbed her laughingly on the head, and helped her off the stool. Yokho set the paint and needles over against the wall. Young Kaka was to receive a tattoo spot on every joint tonight, for he had been Striker in Wohtillin's boat and struck his first whale. It was Yokho's work to give these marks to all the hunters, for their first whale, first polar bear, first mukluk, and for the first funeral they helped with. If they did not have these marks, they would grow stiff in the joints as they grew older. Only a few months before, she had tattooed the marks at each of Tongyan's lip corners which signified he had lost a brother or sister, when they had realized that the six hunters, drifted away on the ice, would never be seen again. Tongyan had had to become a hunter while still a small boy, to take Kulukhon's place.

Walla and the rest still sat, chewing and sewing, and little Enook had disappeared under his mother's parka for a meal. At the far end of the village there was a sudden outbreak of voices. The women all stopped work and looked. Here came the three boys who had gone bird netting that morning, running fast, and at their heels Apangalook and Wohtillin and the whole village. Before they had even reached the house, the women were hurrying to join them and run toward the west beach, for they had heard in all the yammer of voices, "Ungiak, ungiak!"

Enook found himself far away from his warm meal, riding along on his mother's neck again, too surprised to cry.

The ungiak was near, the crew paddling fast, but the surf was running. "They will have to come in with a stern anchor," said Wohtillin, "but they are friends, see how they signal; and the boat is the kind our people over there build."

Even as he spoke the man in the stern threw over a big rock on a line, and with that steadying the stern, the crew pushed in skillfully on a big wave and held the boat steady as that wave receded. Then out of the bow jumped a tall, slim figure, waist deep into the water. He hung onto the boat's bow and ran onto the beach. And just then Okoma cried out in an awful, broken scream, "Toozak!" and turned and ran sobbing aloud back up the shore, back to Apangalook's house.

There was then only stillness as the strange boat's crew pulled it up beyond the waves, up toward the people standing there, dumb.

For it *was* Toozak, and not only Toozak, but Pungwi, and Kulukhon, and Timkaroo, all in strange clothing from across the water, but still unmistakably Timkaroo and Pungwi, still Kulukhon and Toozak, themselves, in their own flesh, looking almost the same as on that day nearly two years before.

Tokoya and Ega were both screaming by now, and running, and Apangalook found a voice at last—a voice hoarse and choked, but a voice. "It seems that unbelievable things do sometimes come to pass," he said, and with arms outstretched, walked toward his two sons who had been gone forever, and were come home again.

CHAPTER XXVI

Their Story

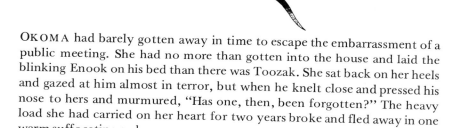

OKOMA had barely gotten away in time to escape the embarrassment of a public meeting. She had no more than gotten into the house and laid the blinking Enook on his bed than there was Toozak. She sat back on her heels and gazed at him almost in terror, but when he knelt close and pressed his nose to hers and murmured, "Has one, then, been forgotten?" The heavy load she had carried on her heart for two years broke and fled away in one warm suffocating rush.

Now, in Wohtillin's house, the men were being fed. From every house in the village, the women hurried with delicacies of every kind they could find, and the whole village had crowded in there and around the doorway to watch them eat, these four returned from the dead, and the four good friends from across the water who had brought them home.

There was hardly a sound of breathing in the room, so closely were they all listening to Pungwi, the oldest of the four, the one to speak.

"So the families of Iyakatan and Ikmallowa need not fear for them. They have gone to the happy world of good spirits." Apangalook bent his head, and everyone looked politely away from him. Pungwi went on.

"For yet many sleeps after that, while the moon turned away and toward us again, we drifted on, farther westward and farther south, until one day we felt the ice had stopped, and when the fog lifted, we were close to some land, and the floe we were on had met the shore ice. We had by that time eaten the last of the walrus and for many days had had only strips of old hide to chew on. But we had strength to hurry on to that land!"

Pungwi paused, remembering. Every hunter in the room was feeling within himself the wonderful feeling those four had had when they at last stepped off that ice and onto land again.

"When we walked up the shore, Toozak was strongest. He found tracks of people, and we followed these, and saw ahead of us two hunters dressed in furs but of strange style. I knew then that we must be in the country of the Chukchee people, and I remembered that Iyakatan had told about someone who had journeyed far and met these people. So when they saw us and stopped, looking at us, I held out my empty hands and called, "Ivokia-meet,"[1] which I had heard was their name for the people of Sevuokuk. We then all sat down, for we had no strength to walk further."

"The two Chukchees came up to us and talked a great deal in their strange words. They understood how we had come there. One of them had a gutskin pouch of seal oil and he poured this into some snow and mixed it up and offered us this to eat. It was not good, but we ate some, and finding friends had given us new strength. We knew we were not to die, after all, and we went on with them to their village. There they had only dried fish—they do not have the wealth of food we have here, but we were fed, and given clothing and skins and treated as friends."

Pungwi looked about the crowd of still, eager faces, faces of his own people, his own wife and sons, all gazing at him (except Okoma and Tokoya and Ega, who could only gaze at their husbands), all hanging on his words. A great day, this, in the life of Pungwi the whale Striker. "Of course, the first thing we did when we had strength was to offer our ceremony of thanksgiving. In the dump pile of the Chukchee village we all rolled for many minutes."

He stopped and reached into the big platter once more and crammed some freshly boiled auklet into his mouth. He could not tell the whole great story in a breath. It had taken two years for all this to happen. One could not be expected to spit it all out in one mouthful!

They all waited quietly; the four young strangers were busy picking choice bits of seal flippers from a platter. Gently, Wohtillin asked, "And all that summer, and last winter?"

"We were traveling along the shores of that big country, by boat and on foot, in whatever way we could, trying to reach the part of the country where our friends and relatives live. We reached there late last summer, too late to cross over here by boat, so we had to stay there all winter, waiting to come home."

Apangalook leaned forward, looking with joy in his eyes at Toozak and Timkaroo, "Surely this is the greatest story the people of Sevuokuk have ever known."

There were quick sighs and murmurs all about the room. "Many strange things we saw across there," went on Pungwi, and his round face was full of smiles again. "Oktohok, here, can tell you what things have come to their homes in the last few moons."

Oktohok was square of face and body and his hair was heavy below his tonsure and hung almost to his eyes, and he also had hair growing on his upper lip, as so many of the people from across the water had. He licked the seal oil from his fingers and began to speak, looking at Wohtillin and Apangalook, as the important men among his hosts.

"There have come to our shores such Ungiakpuk as would hold all the ungiaks of your village. These fly over the water by use of wind and great sails. They are manned by a people of great strength and size but with no color in their skins. We call them 'Laluremka'."

"Ah-h," said Wohtillin, "such a boat and such people appeared here once many, many moons ago, but our people hid from it; it seemed too strange, almost like a sorcerer's dream."

"Ah, no," laughed Oktohok, "they are not a dream. We have known of such boats for years, but now they come every year. They come only to catch whales and you would perhaps not believe me when I tell you how they catch them."

Oktohok paused, shook his head. Apangalook spoke, "The word of a welcome guest is never doubted."

So Oktohok spoke very slowly, that they might all understand. "The big boats have many small ones, and in these they chase the whale, as we do, but the strange thing is that their harpoons come flying out of a black thing which the Striker holds against his shoulder, and when the harpoon head has flown into the whale, they say it flies all to pieces, and this soon brings death to Ahgvook."

Oktohok sighed, "One could never be finished, were he to tell all the wonderful things these Laluremka keep in their boats. They seem to need a great many things in order to live. More than floating ningloos, these Ungiakpuk are. Your Toozak, here, was on one of these boats. He can tell you about them—when he has time!"

Oktohok added this last, slyly, and everyone laughed loud and long; it was a good excuse for the laughter which had been welling up in them all. For it was plain to see that their Toozak had time for nothing but Okoma now. Forgetful of all etiquette, they sat close together, not even knowing what went on, but joining gaily in the loud laughter at their own expense.

Ah yes, indeed, Toozak was home! They had not realized how somber these years had been, until they heard once more his laugh ringing out above all the others. Toozak and happiness, back home on Sevuokuk again!

CHAPTER XXVII

Ungiakpuk Again

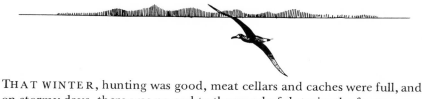

THAT WINTER, hunting was good, meat cellars and caches were full, and on stormy days, there was no end to the wonderful stories the four returned from the great adventure could tell in the houses about the lamps. They danced through many of the long nights, and in February, the moon of young seals, Wohtillin and Apangalook together had a great festival of giving, to show their thanks for the return of Kulukhon and Toozak and Timkaroo. All the able-bodied of Kukulik came with their dog teams, even Walanga and his stout Kooungo. For many days and nights the houses were full of talk and laughter and great eating. The village was full of smiling faces; those sad times were quickly forgotten.

That next summer brought again the Ungiakpuk to Sevuokuk. This time the people did not run and hide. They watched the two tall things come to rest, far out from shore, and Toozak led a procession of ungiaks from the village to see these things close up.

The women and children sat on the shore and watched. Walla and Assoonga and all the rest held their sewing in their laps, but there were very few stitches going into summer boots or rain parkas or sealskin pants. Their eyes must return always to the big ships, and what might be going on out there.

After a long time they saw their own people coming back, but behind them were other ungiaks, strange, smooth-looking ones. "The Laluremka are coming ashore, too," cried Tokoya, jumping to her feet.

Quick as dolphins they gathered their sewing and scrambled up. For women to face these strange beings was not to be thought of. Away to Apangalook's house they ran. It was the nearest to the landing place, and besides, no one could think of leaving the group and going to her own house in such an excitement. The children ran like young sandpipers and tumbled into the doorway.

Only old Yokho, being the oldest woman and afraid of nothing, could properly stay outside. Near the doorway she sat, shredding a piece of sinew but watching all that went on. The rest of them huddled inside, near enough to the opening to hear Yokho's voice.

"They have all come ashore," she murmured, head down. "Now they are at Apangalook's meat rack. Toozak is going up. He is passing the baleen down. Ah-k—they are taking it all down. Down to the boats they go with it. They are taking it out to the Ungiakpuk. Ah-k—what kinds of things have I lived to see!" Yokho snapped a loop of sinew and spat.

Walla leaned out; she was curious. "Why do you speak so, Yokho?"

Yokho shaded her eyes and looked after the boats; all the Sevuokuk boats were going back out to the big ships, too. "I cannot tell—but something does not feel right to me. I cannot feel any good in the air these pale men breathe."

Now the doorway was full of women, watching the boats, listening to Yokho. "Yes, they have changed the air of Sevuokuk. They do not belong here. There is something not good." Yokho sat there, muttering.

But these words were forgotten when the men of the village came back and each spread out his treasures. The strangers were very kind, that was plain to be seen, for the baleen had been paid for with such wonderful things from the land of the Laluremka as Inuit eyes had never beheld.

On a big skin in front of Wohtillin's house the men spread these things, and the women and children crouched and gazed in awe. Needles of a stuff that shone like sun on the water; tiny boxes or dishes of this same marvelous substance, and some of these dishes had bright colored covers around them of a skin even thinner than intestine leather. There was also a new kind of food; flat round things, white. They had no taste, but they were fun to chew.

But, next to the needles, the best things of all were the beads, some colored like the summer sky, some like the parka-hood flowers growing on the spit; all so much more beautiful than any ivory ones. Kulukhon had gotten a handful for Tokoya, and she was already stringing them on a sinew string to be braided through her hair, rolling the smooth things in her fingers and rubbing them against her cheek.

Another wonderful thing was a new kind of skin; the men said it was to make summer clothing from, but it had no warmth, only beautiful colors, some like blood and some like the sand flowers at the big lagoon and some like the crest of an auklet. But Yokho made a face as she flipped a corner of it over; it had no more feel to it than the skin of a baby seagull.

It took all that day to look at new property. Pungwi himself had the strangest thing of all, which he said the leader of the Laluremka had given him. It was a poke made of the same kind of stone that was once in a great while found on the beach, which fell from the sky and was kept in charm bags and which could be seen through. This poke was as big as a mukluk bladder and held water which could clearly be seen through the wonderful stone. Pungwi tipped it back and forth so that Sekwo and the other children could see it swirling about inside. He said that he had heard over in the old land, which these Laluremka called 'Siberia,' that the water from these pokes was hot without being heated, and that it gave one a dream better than wapacha.

Yokho sat and shook her head. She was sure Iyakatan would not have approved of all this. She kept on shaking her head several days later when the Ungiakpuk sailed on north after whales, and took with them Kulukhon and Tokoya, Toozak and Okoma, and the two young daughters of Ungalik of Kukulik. It seemed the white men wanted plenty of women along to make skin clothing for them, and Yokho could see that the young women's heads were full of dreams of many beads and many bright needles, and of course those chosen to go felt honored, and superior to all the stay-at-homes; though why Ungalik's young girls should be chosen was hard to see, for everyone knew they could not sew fit clothing for a hunter!

. . . . .

The big fall storm was threatening, the south sky was dark and full of wind, when the boats returned. The small smooth-sided boats came ashore in a hurry and the Sevuokuk people who had been away all summer climbed out of them. A white hunter carried Ungalik's Kargew through the surf in his arms, and she squealed loud and clung to him, for all the people to see, and then she and her sister began greeting everyone in loud voices, before any of the men had spoken. Walla turned to Rohltungu, "It may be as well we did not go with the strangers. We would not have learned any manners, it seems."

Queer things, indeed, were happening these days. Yokho was glad when the last scraps of baleen in the village, and much ivory, had been taken out to the big boats and they had sailed away, flying fast in the strong wind, but she knew they would be back every year. It appeared that things had to be different on Sevuokuk from now on.

Timkaroo and Kulukhon and Toozak had much to tell about. Toozak could not help feeling he was a little wiser now than people who had known only Sevuokuk all their days. Yet he was glad to return to the home beaches. The Laluremka expected a man to be a little too generous with the loan of his wife. Both he and Okoma were glad to be back in their own house, with all that behind them. And still there were days when Toozak felt no laughter pushing up through his throat. He and Kulukhon had with them many pokes of the dreaming water, but it did not seem to make them any stronger. When they ran the circle in the mornings they were always the last ones in, and Toozak could lift only half the big stones he had lifted before he went away with the white men. Sometimes he wondered about this . . .

One evening he sat at the council rocks, watching Kulukhon and the other young men running around the rocks, jumping over them. Kulukhon reached the last stone, but fell there, gasping and moaning, his strength gone. Wohtillin and Apangalook sat on the big stone near Toozak, and they were all silent for a long time. Finally Apangalook spoke, in a slow, heavy way, "Some fine things we have gotten from the white whale hunters, but it may be that what is good for them is not so good for Inuit. This strong water is not like wapacha, leaving a man well again when it passes over, but like a sickness leaving one weak. I see no good thing about it. Look, here is Pungwi's Tatoowi now, having this kind of dream, out here at the council rocks instead of quietly on his robes as he would be with wapacha."

Tatoowi came staggering up to the rocks, shouting in a hoarse voice not like his own. He fell onto one of the rocks and waved his poke of dream water at Tongyan and Kaka. They drank too, and tried to sing, but fell to laughing. Tatoowi rolled over and over on the gravel, and reached for the poke. They were feeling so happy; the white men had certainly brought great joy to Sevuokuk.

Pungwi came along the beach, and went to Tatoowi and touched him on the shoulder, "Do you not know that the current has slackened at the cape and the young hunters should be out with the seal nets?"

Tatoowi looked up at his father, squinted his eyes as though he could not see, smiled and then laughed, and, bracing himself on the rock, pushed at Pungwi and kept on laughing. Pungwi bowed his head and walked away. The others sitting there could not speak. They had never seen a thing like this—a son laying a hand on his father, refusing to follow a father's word! It had never been thought of. Tatoowi's voice came to them high and wild. "Speak not of seal netting. What care we for that now? We shall sit here and laugh and have joy we never knew before. Seals may be netted any time," and he rolled to the ground and held the wonderful drink up to Kaka's outstretched hand, and they were still laughing as Pungwi walked slowly home.

But Toozak sat there when the older men had gone to their beds, when his friend Tatoowi and the other young ones had staggered away. The surf was rolling in stronger and stronger with the tide. The late gulls flew screaming back and forth above the white lines of foam. There was no other sound; the sky was dark and so was Toozak's heart. "I am beginning to believe old Yokho," he thought, "perhaps she is the wisest as well as the oldest. The things of Laluremka have changed the laughter of this village."

If he could only feel joy rushing up in him as it had before! Two years of being lost on the ice, and in strange far countries had not killed it, but the things of the Laluremka—what were they doing to them all?

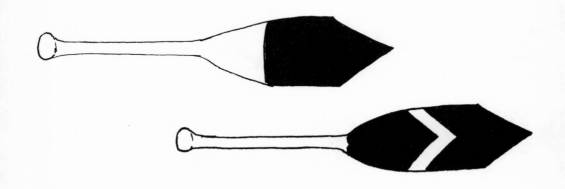

CHAPTER XXVIII

The Year 1878

THE LALUREMKA had come every year for a long time now. Everyone
was older. Little Sekwo had been old enough to go north with the big boats
that spring, and Yokho was so old she sat most of the time in a corner,
talking softly to herself and shredding sinew. She could no longer chew
mukluk for boots.

One big ship had stayed around Sevuokuk all this summer and, when it
left in the fall, took all the baleen and much ivory. Some food the people
got from the ship, and some of the shiny things the white men kept certain
food in, which they called 'cans' (pieces of these made fine charms to wear)
and knives, and many beads for the women (it was said that Ungalik of
Kukulik, who had so much baleen and ivory to trade, had bought a whole
great box of beads for his young wife). But the most amazing things were
the queer weapons that Laluremka had sold to them, heavy black things
which they could point at the birds. When a certain part of this thing was
pressed, a horrible noise came out, all the children screamed, and everyone
ran, and the birds fell dead. It was altogether too strange to understand, but
they said many birds could be taken this way.

More than all else, they had the dreaming water the Laluremka called
'whiskey.'

The fall worships were big festivals this year, for they had some of the
strange food of the white men left, and plenty of the strange drink, so that
the men thought of nothing but joy. Of course, old Yokho sat and
muttered and shook her head, and Massiu told of more queer dreams he had
been having, and Wohtillin complained that with all the queer new hunting
gear, there were not enough dried auklets in seal oil, and too little mangona
put away for the early winter, not even the cormorants they usually had in

205

the fall.

Toozak would not drink or join with them in the great fun, going out hunting alone every day instead, but no one listened much to all this, and no one else went out hunting.

Then came Akomak, the moon of sitting, with snow flying thick before a fierce southeast wind. The worships were over and the whiskey gone. The hunters were all very tired, somehow, and no one should expect them to go out in such storms.

. . . . .

Okoma was suddenly awake. She rose on an elbow and looked about the house. The lamp was trimmed very low, for they were running out of oil, but she could see the sleeping faces of her family, Toozak beside her, Enook and Sekwo. She looked toward Assoonga's corner and saw that she, too, was sitting up and her face had lost its calm look. The storm was shaking the very walls, screaming in every crack and throwing loose snow and gravel clear over the roof. Okoma shivered, and spoke softly, "Assoonga, what is it?"

Assoonga moaned, "Ah-k, this is no common storm. The souls of all those up there on the mountain are come back to cry around this village tonight."

Yokho, from her place near the entrance, now began to chant, and Assoonga, she who, through every other happening, had been the calm one, now rocked herself back and forth and began, too, chanting aloud the secret family formulas against evil, passed to her from her forefathers. Toozak awoke at this and sat up and looked wide-eyed at his mother. Enook cried out in his sleep, and Apangalook threw back his robes and reached for his parka. Then it came.

A low roar far away, growing and deepening and traveling nearer, until it was among them, moving the very ground beneath the house, shaking the boards of the outer wall with a fierce scraping and creaking, while every dog in the village howled. The storm never slackened. The clay cooking pot hanging over the lamp began swinging back and forth; Sekwo pointed at it with a shaking finger, and all the women cried aloud.

Like men in a dream, Apangalook and Toozak and Timkaroo pulled on their boots. The shaking died a little as they pulled at them, then came again. They ran through the passageway, and looked out into the terrible night. A shadowy something came reeling through the flying snow—Massiu.

"Look down at the shore," he screamed at them, and his voice was trembling.

The horrible roar came again, under and yet above the crash of breakers, and on the shore, from among the jumbled rocks, came jets of blue fire. Even through the blown snow, Toozak and the others saw them plainly and felt the anger of all the spirits flung at them through the night. Toozak had lived through much, but one could never dream of anything like this. It had never been told of, even in the stories of the oldest people. When the roaring and shaking died away they were all trembling from head to foot, and they crept back into the warm house among the crying women and lay breathing heavily, saying nothing.

· · · · ·

Toozak and Pungwi stood on Sevuokuk's mountain top among the big rocks again, and looked to the north. No glint of Siko, no whiteness in the sky, only cold gray waves and heavy dark sky and the south wind whistling in their ears and moaning in the rock crevices and filling the air with snow. Pungwi turned back to the rocky slope—he was tired and hungry, too. "Perhaps Yokho spoke truth," he said. "We drank and made festival like Laluremka. Now perhaps we shall go hungry like Inuit."

Down in the village they met Kulukhon and Timkaroo, dragging their feet heavily through the snow. Their seal nets hung over their shoulders but their baleen toboggans were empty. The breakers and the strong current off the cape defeated them every day. No one had caught a seal for weeks. For weeks before that, no one had hunted except Toozak, and now it was almost the moon of young seals and still Siko had not come. The south wind still blew. Toozak's seals had all been divided among the people and his family were all as hungry as any of them now.

The north wind *must* come, or all of Sevuokuk would be an empty place. It was the same all over the island. While Toozak and Pungwi stood on the Cape Mountain at Sevuokuk village, far across, beyond Kukulik village, the breakers were roaring at the foot of the high cliffs and tossing spray far over the top, and Koonooku, head man of Kukulik, giver of great festivals, knelt there. He was drenched with spray, but still he knelt and pounded on the big rock at the cliff top and sang for the north wind—sang and sang.

Koonooku sang for the north wind and the ice and food. He sang with awful fear in his heart; tears rolled over his cheeks. The south wind smashed the breakers against the cliff and showered him again with icy coldness.

. . . . .

The people of Powooiliak, that place of bears which Toozak had discovered and some of Pungwi's brothers had settled in in the old days, had not traded with the Ungiakpuk that year. They had no whiskey, and the current and the breakers were not so strong down there, so they had netted many seals in the fall. Kulukhon had gone with Wohtillin's dogteam and brought back seal meat and oil from Soworak, brother of Pungwi. But Koonooku and many others had come with scrawny dog teams from Kukulik and the seal meat had to be divided among them. They were sad people, those Kukulik people. They had had even less in their meat cellars than Sevuokuk village when the fall storms came. They had many big pokes of whiskey. Three had died on the way to Sevuokuk, and surely there was very little help or cheer to be found when they got there.

Koonooku and his people started home with some of the seal meat. Toozak helped them start their poor dogs, stood and watched them go struggling up the slope beyond the lake, and wondered if they would come again when the yellow flowers would bloom by the lake and the sandpipers circle above it. Who would there be to net the first auklets?

He looked up and down the shore. No living thing could be seen. The southeast wind which had mocked and screamed during three moons still romped and flung spray and gravel over the beaches and made a continual song of anger and grief and warning over the quiet village. Toozak went slowly to the meat cellar. It was hard, just walking, these days. Down at the bottom of the cellar lay one small seal, already skinned and with most of the blubber gone. Toozak pulled it up and was surprised at how heavy it was; it must be a very heavy seal for its size; he had almost to drag it over to the doorsill. Just then the hungry sad-eyed dogs lying at the back of the house set up a quick yelping. A dog team was coming.

Toozak paused, the seal hanging over the sill, and watched the team coming at a fast trot from down the shore. The dogs looked lively and well fed, and the driver sprang lightly from the sled at Apangalook's door. "Hah, Toozak, it seems a traveler sometimes finds a very quiet village."

Toozak only gazed dumbly at the visitor. Here was Kastevik, his good friend and cousin from Punuk Island, far across the Island and east of it, and they could offer him no warmth of welcome, no feast of friendship, no sharing of adventures and light, contented laughter in a warm house. Kastevik must have come in a straight line from Punuk, behind the mountains of Kukulik, and so not have heard the sad news.

"Ah, Kastevik, welcome we should give a visitor, but we have nothing to offer a guest, neither of food nor good talk. You have traveled long miles to come to a sad village."

Kastevik was hungry. He had traveled hard. But he tried to eat very little of the boiled seal meat which Assoonga chopped up in the long platter, and he brought in the bag of frozen mangona he had in his sled, and pounded a little of the blubber himself in Assoonga's stone blubber dish for Enook. Okoma smiled at him with tears running down her face when he brought in the blubber.

That night the storm increased and shook the houses and tossed snow and spray over them as though it could never be through tormenting Sevuokuk. And Kastevik, who had come from a full meat cellar into famine, who had come to buy more sled dogs from his cousins, found himself tied there in those sad, silent houses, by a storm too fierce to allow the thought of travel.

On the third night, Kastevik was wakened by the fierce howling of a dog just outside the walls, but the dog's voice suddenly ceased, almost as though he had been choked. Kastevik did not go out to see what the trouble was. Going out would chill him through, and Apangalook's house, with one feeble flame burning, was hardly warm enough to sleep in as it was.

In the morning the wind had become a little tired, at last, and Toozak and Timkaroo and the rest of Apangalook's boat crew got the boat into the water and set out to net seals. Very slowly they went, their arms heavy as though hung with rocks, and Apangalook knew they could not go far or stay out long, because their paddles could not meet the waves. Toozak saw strong young Kaka bite his lips and stroke desperately, sweat pouring down his cheeks. There was no strength in his own arms, and a wave of weakness rolled over him from head to foot. He wanted to roll into the bottom of the boat but he knew he must sit up and try, and there was no way to stop the tears which brimmed over his eyelids.

There were no seals that day.

. . . . .

Kastevik went out to hitch up his dogs. Perhaps he could get back home in this lull in the storm, although the sky was still dark, with clouds racing high, and of course he had no food to take with him. Behind the house where he had left his dogs there were only two of Apangalook's bony things lying there hopelessly, about to breathe their last.

Then he remembered the night and the choked howl of a dog. He stood there in the cold wind, and the coldness pierced clear through him. He looked up through the line of houses, but he knew he was lost. It would be of no use to search; he knew how hungry the people were.

. . . . .

After a while there were no dogs left. It had been weeks since anyone had had strength enough to hitch up a team to hunt for a fox or a ptarmigan inland, and all the dogs had to be eaten. Kastevik's were the first because they were fat, but after that, they were glad to have any kind, and finally it must be eaten raw, for there was only enough seal oil left to keep a few houses warmer than outdoors, and in these few, everyone huddled together. It seemed there was no longer heat in human bodies to warm a small house.

Tokoya had found a piece of walrus hide on the sleeping platform and was cutting it into strips with fumbling strokes of her oolak. Okoma lay on a deerskin robe, holding little Kofkok to her breast; no one had strength to sit up longer. Kofkok was Tatoowi's son; his wife, Asha, of Kukulik, had quietly fled her body the day before, and Okoma still strove to keep life in the baby. She took the piece of hide Tokoya handed her and put one end of it into her mouth to suck it. She had no power in her jaws to chew the tough skin. Tokoya passed strips of hide to all the others in the room, all lying close to one another for warmth. Assoonga still murmured formulas, but the rest had no wish even to speak. One thought was in every mind, and to speak it would be to loose it among them and hasten the end.

Little Kofkok cried one weak sad wail and his head rolled back on Okoma's arm. His soul had gone. Okoma hid her face on the thin little bundle and her body shook. Sweet Okoma, she felt that all there was left of her was a thin shell holding a great heavy hopelessness. She saw Tatoowi raise his head and look, and drop down again, hands over his face. He was a hunter who could find no food for his family—nothing could be worse. Old Yokho was gone, she who had warned them all, and young Okohoni, and many from other families. Even those who still had a little food left were dying in the terrible pains of a strange sickness. Now, Tatoowi's son. Okoma looked fearfully over at her own Enook, and at Sekwo, lying heavy-eyed, the skin tight over their bones. And where could Toozak, her brave one, be? He had crawled out of the house hours before.

There was a shout from outside the house—a feeble shout, but everyone in the agra sat up and stared as though roused from death. Again came the call, "Siko, Siko! Iviek!"

Siko! They had been thinking it would never come again, that it had never been, and now it had come, too late perhaps. But Pungwi and Tatoowi crawled out to the door, Kulukhon and Apangalook after them, and found Toozak leaning against the entrance, calling and pointing.

The ice had come, but could they do anything about it? The great white field was coming nearer and nearer, but the shore ice reached out only a little way, because the storms had kept breaking it up. The floe would have to come close. Pungwi was pointing to a blackness on the floe, a herd of Iviek, perhaps a hundred of them, lying far out of reach of starving people. Kulukhon put his arm over his eyes, but Wohtillin's mouth was hard. "When the ice is fastened on, we will have to try."

And that was how Pungwi, the round-cheeked smiling one, lost his life upon an ice floe after all, and with him Kastevik of Punuk Island, and Tatoowi. (Yes, Tatoowi, lively companion of Toozak's youth. He paid now for all his joy in fiery water.) Get Iviek they did, and crawling and falling and groaning, dragged it piece by piece to the shore ice, where Toozak, too weak to stand, knelt and cut it up and somehow divided it among the people. The hunters went back for the last slab, and were dragging it slowly along, crawling on their hands and knees. Then there came a loud crack and a roar, and a great piece of ice broke from the shore ice, loosened by the swift current, and moved out. There were the five hunters on the moving floe, and there were their people to whom they had just brought food, kneeling on the shore. The hunters lifted their arms once, that was all. They knew no one could help them this time.

Toozak, the laughing one, hid his face in his hands and felt all laughter die in him. Tatoowi, his friend, who had been with him on so many happy days, Kastevik, his cousin, and Pungwi who had helped him live through all that bad dream on that other ice floe—they were all going from his sight.

Walla bowed her head and crawled back over the snow. Assoonga came with a piece of fresh mangona, but Walla shook her head, "Keep it for the young ones. I am going; perhaps I shall reach the spirit world before Pungwi does. Already I feel the pains of the sickness in my body. Yokho spoke truth. The ways of Laluremka are not for Inuit. Now there is food, and the people still die. There is no end to the evil that strange drink brought us."

Walla crept into Apangalook's house with Toozak and Okoma, and Okoma put some of the fresh blubber into the lamp to make it warmer and hung a pot of meat over it. "Toozak says we must cook the meat well if we would still live."

How blessed the heat was! Yet Walla lay staring before her, feeling nothing. Pungwi, her husband, was really gone this time, and Okohoni, her little son. Only Kaka was left, and he lay beside her, looking as though life were not long for him. No one said anything. After a while Timkaroo began feeding them all some of the broth and meat which had been brought in at such cost. It sent warmth through their limbs again, but they were far from happy people. And with some of them, the fiery pains of the new sickness increased as they swallowed the good food. Walla was soon gone.

One walrus, then the wind came back, and in the days that it roared over the village again, Assoonga gave up living—Assoonga, beloved of everyone, she who had never tired, who had always smiled as she worked. This was the greatest sorrow of all.

The sickness took her and many more, and the living had no strength to drag the dead far toward the mountain. They lay on the snow back of the houses, but there were no dogs to disturb them. Day after day dragged by. Okoma and Sekwo, Ega and Tokoya, they were all like shadows, but life stayed with them, and Timkaroo and Toozak fed them and Enook the last few bits of blubber, the last shreds of mangona.

Toozak was not sure whether he himself were still alive or not; it was all like a wapacha dream, with a mist always before his eyes. His father, after Assoonga went, lay like a ghost, still, as though dead, as though waiting to die.

One walrus would be plenty of food for the whole village now, but not even one walrus could be seen through the thick-blown snow. In Wohtillin's house lay Rohltungu. She was no longer Rohltungu of the bright cheeks and quick smile. She tried not to moan when the pains came, and she had been dead a little while before Wohtillin knew it. He and Tongyan lay with very bright eyes, watching, yet when Wohtillin reached over and touched her, she was already cold.

He and Tongyan had been spared the sickness but they were suffering something worse—the madness of hunger.

Slowly Wohtillin pulled off Rohltungu's clothing; he had so little strength in his hands, but within him a wild spirit that could not be denied cried out constantly for food. Tongyan spoke in a hoarse wild whisper, "Do you remember what Oktohok of Siberia told us about the men of his land, what they did when they had a great hunger time? Surely we shall die if we do not eat soon."

Wohtillin nodded. His hand closed on the good hunting knife in his belt. He had purchased it with four fox skins from the white men. He could not stop his hand now. It reached toward Rohltungu's breasts.

Perhaps this would keep her husband and her son alive a few days longer.

CHAPTER XXIX

Return to Kukulik

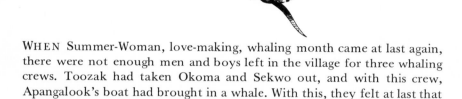

WHEN Summer-Woman, love-making, whaling month came at last again, there were not enough men and boys left in the village for three whaling crews. Toozak had taken Okoma and Sekwo out, and with this crew, Apangalook's boat had brought in a whale. With this, they felt at last that the anger of the spirits must be gone, and that they who were left might begin to think of life again.

Few they were, and when the ice was gone, no one came from Kukulik. Wohtillin and Apangalook, Kaka and Toozak, when they were strong enough, made a journey over there in Wohtillin's ungiak.

When they came to the cliffs above Kukulik, the birds came out to meet them. From the green caves and carved tunnels and arches at the water's edge, and from the ledges and crevices far up the cliff, they came out in murmuring swarms.

The boat passed by and rounded the seal rocks which made a little harbor at Kukulik. Three seals lay sleeping, as though they had never been disturbed, and Apangalook muttered, "Keh-h, it does not look good in this place."

They beached their boat. The boats of the Kukulik people were lashed on their racks. Seagulls screamed and quarreled on all the kelp-covered rocks and rode in on the surf. Snow buntings fluttered and squeaked among the houses, and in the little lake behind the village, phalaropes[1] were busy, going round and round, picking their food from the water.

That was all. No living person came to meet them, only a sikkik poked his head out from under a whale-rib house timber, and told them they did not belong here.

"The wild things have taken this village again as their own," said Apangalook, finally. "People died here, too many of them, and people do not belong here any more."

Apangalook would have gone back to the boat then. Sorrow was still too heavy within him. Assoonga's soul still seemed to hover about him always. But Toozak walked over to the house of Koonooku, their cousin, the great man of Kukulik. The winter roof had been taken off, and beside the winter house the topek frame was up but had not been covered. They had lived through the winter and died in the spring, then, perhaps not so long ago. Toozak stooped and looked into the house, Tongyan close behind him. They saw nothing but a curtain stretched inside, made of walrus-stomach boat sails.

In the queer-smelling darkness, Toozak pulled that thin curtain aside. There lay what had been seven strong young Inuit—Koonooku and his youngest wife, her sister, and four children. Toozak and Tongyan stood there frozen. How they longed to be out of that place, but their limbs had turned to water. Wohtillin's voice helped them; he leaned through the door. "Come, this is of no use, looking at our friends who are gone. They have gone to a good spirit place and we cannot touch anything here. It is certain they starved." He pointed to the row of clay bowls turned upside down along the wall, the sign of famine.

Toozak and Tongyan took up their paddles with trembling hands and shoved away through the surf like men possessed of a strange spirit. No one suggested trying to sneak up on the seals, still sleeping there on the rocks. They paddled as hard as they could, and Toozak knew that none of them would ever visit Kukulik again as long as they lived. It now belonged to the dead, that place which had seen so many festivals. He knew that with the years the snow buntings would build nests in every hollow whale rib and no person would disturb them.

CHAPTER XXX

End and Beginning

THE MOON turned its face again toward them and brought the warm days of Penahvek. Fog and mist rolled away, and there were days that almost made them forget cold and famine and biting winds and emptiness of houses.

Wohtillin fastened a rock to the last lashing of the topek roof and looked out over the water. Clouds of puffins and murres were skimming over the waves, but no boat was to be seen. Toozak and Apangalook had gone on a long journey. They all knew they must have more people on Sevuokuk, and these two strong ones had gone across to the Siberian villages to bring back new wives, new hunters, new families.

Wohtillin picked up a piece of ivory and sat down in the sun to carve a bird dart. The sawbills and geese were flying noisily over, and from the lake came the chatter of sandpipers and plovers. Not far away sat Kaka, stringing his eider snares.

The snare Kaka made was a short stick, with a hole drilled in one end. Through this hole he slipped two loop snares of thin baleen. Kaka had many of these snares, and when they were all strung on a small mukluk rope he slung them over his shoulder and walked across the spit to the lake.

On the bank above the lake, Kaka lay on his belly and slid along through the strong-smelling funeral plant and the purple July flowers and peeked over onto the lake shore. Eiders[1] , a family of them, were swimming silently about. Kaka smiled, "Ah, you quiet ones. You no doubt think I cannot see you because you are so quiet."

Cautiously Kaka slid down onto the mud and slipped his sticks off their rope. Here and there over the mud he stuck the sharp sticks, so that only the snares showed above the mud; then, quiet as an eider himself, he crept

217

back up and lay in the grass. He had plenty of time. Sooner or later the eiders would come walking and walk right into the baleen loops of his snares, and eiders were very good to eat at this time of year. How good they would have been in those dark days of the moons of seals! That day in the ungiak when he could no longer lift his paddle, that darkest day of all when his jolly mother Walla had gone, when Pungwi went slipping away on the ice again—Ahk, he must not think of those days now. They were gone, and all they must remember of them was that the white men's drink was not for the people of Sevuokuk.

Kaka shook his head and blinked, looked about at the bright day, pushed those dark hours out of his head. He pulled a handful of nunivak from beside him and lay chewing and half dreaming, fed and content and safe once more. Voices came from the mountainside above him. The few women and children left on Sevuokuk were up there in the sunshine, gathering nunivak. The children were rolling down the little mossy terraces of the mountain, laughing and poking their mouths full of green cloudberries, greens, every kind of thing which looked good to eat. Their cheeks were round and smooth again.

Far up the slope Kaka saw Sekwo, gathering greens alone. He remembered that eider snares really didn't need watching. The ducks, once caught, couldn't get away. He started aimlessly up the slope, peering under rock jumbles and examining every squirrel hole as though out looking for fox holes for next winter's trapping. Somehow he found himself near the top of the mountain, where Sekwo stooped very busily in a patch of greens, alone.

Kaka for a moment remembered how drawn and gray and old Sekwo had seemed, as they all had, that day they had brought in the big whale, and life had begun again. He gazed at her now while retying his boot string. For some reason, he and Sekwo, playmates in childhood, had both lived through all the awful days. Now youth and strength and warm sunshine were come back again.

Her braids hung shiny black on each side of her rounded cheeks, and the cheeks had some bright color like the flowers of Penahvek in them, and her eyes were very black again. Best of all, her nose was so small and lovable. Kaka spoke indifferently, "Your poke seems almost full. You would not be needing any help, I suppose?"

Sekwo looked up as though much surprised to see him there. "What! Does the mighty hunter come to nunivak-picking with women?"

"With only one woman, I think," answered Kaka. "It sometimes happens that a hunter needs a woman."

He shoved a handful of nunivak into the poke very carefully. Sekwo had no words for this. It was no customary thing going on here; a man talking thus openly with a woman, even though their marriage had been agreed on before by their parents, before all the sad days came. But then, those sad days had changed many things.

Kaka was still picking greens. Sekwo hesitated, kneeling beside the poke. "What does a hunter do, then, when he needs a woman?" she murmured very low.

Kaka smiled, and Kaka was very good to look at when he smiled. "He sometimes comes in the darkness and takes her. At least, I have heard people tell of such things. And when a man's clothing looks like this, surely he needs a woman?"

Sekwo looked Kaka up and down. Tall he was now, and slender, like Toozak. What a fine looking hunter she could make of him! Now his cormorant-skin parka was not only torn but almost worn bare in places, and one boot had a great rip in the side. Her fingers fairly itched for sinew and her bright new needles, but she collected herself quickly. "It is quite probable that my father and brother, when they return from over there, will have some very good sewing women with them."

"Ah yes, no doubt," answered Kaka. "I have heard Toozak say those women are very quick and clever with a needle." He thought to himself— "There, answer that, you smart little woman."

But Sekwo did not answer. She who had always been so quick to answer when they had been children together, gave him one look from her bright eyes and then looked intently out toward the white Siberian mountains. She knew the hunter would be coming in the darkness that very night. *He* knew that she would be lying wide awake in the darkness, waiting.

Now there was something else. Sekwo pointed suddenly across the water. Bright, bright blue it lay, quiet as the sky, and on its blueness were black dots. Kaka and Sekwo stood together in the bright flowers, with the snow buntings darting about over their heads, the blue sky hot upon them, and watched. There were four black dots, which soon grew to be ungiaks, full of people, and they came swiftly toward the shore and the landing place below the village.

A beautiful sight that was, on this still, bright day; those brown boats gliding over the blue water to Sevuokuk. Toozak was coming home again, bringing with him new life for the island, and the island was smiling in its best garments to receive him!

Kaka laughed aloud. He knew Toozak would be laughing again, now. So would they all. He pulled a clump of red flowers from the moss and flung them into the air and laughed, and Sekwo turned to him, and laughed, too.

It was the first time they had felt joy rise up in them and burst forth since the moon Akomak. Suddenly, they both realized that they could still feel light and warm inside.

And so, laughing, they went leaping and running down the mountain, side by side, and from the first ungiak riding in upon the surf below, Toozak's laughing shout came up to them!

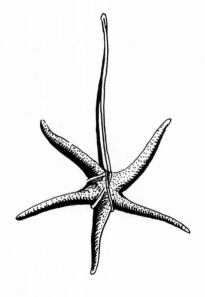

NOTES

PREFACE   1. Archeological Excavations at Kukulik, St. Lawrence Island, Alaska. U.S. Government Printing Office, Washington D.C., 1936.

CHAPTER II   1. Ribbon seal *Phoca fasciata*

CHAPTER XII   1. Red-breasted merganser *Mergus serrator*
2. Least Auklet *Aethia pusilla*
3. Fulmar *Fulmarus g. rodgersi*

CHAPTER XIV   1. Longspur: Alaska Longspur *Calcarius lapponicus alascensis*

CHAPTER XVI   1. Sandpipers: The common resident sandpiper is the Aleutian Sandpiper *Calidris ptilocnemis.*
2. Jaeger: Three jaegers occur on the Island, Pomarine *Stercorarius pomarinus,* Parasitic *S. parasiticus,* and Long-tailed *S. longicaudus*
3. Cloudberry *Rubus chamaemorus*
4. Snow bunting *Plectrophenax nivalis nivalis*
5. Red mice: Red-backed mouse *Clethrionomys albiventer*
6. *Oxyria diagyna* (L.) Hill and *Saxifraga nelsoniana* D. Don
7. Bistort *Polygonum bistortoides* Pursh.
8. Blossom of *Saxifraga nelsoniana* D. Don
9. Ground squirrel *Citellus lyratus*
10. Gentians *Gentiana frigida* Haenke
11. The song, still sung to this day on the island, "another point, still another point in the way." They have such respect for the ocean that they never steer a course from point to point, but follow quite close to the shore all the way.
12. Ground vine: Crowberry *Empetrum nigrum*

CHAPTER XVII   1. Alder bark

CHAPTER XVIII   1. Guillemot: Pigeon guillemot *Cepphus columba*
                               2. Petrel: Forked-tailed Petrel *Oceanodroma furcata*
                               3. Murre: Pallas Murre *Uria lomvia arra*.
                                  The California Murre *Uria a. californica*,
                                  is also found on the Island.

CHAPTER XXII   1. Sage *Artemisia tilesii Isdeb*

CHAPTER XXIII   1. A species of lamprey
                               2. Leafy kelp *Laminaria sp*.
                               3. Green seaweed *Ulva sp*.
                               4. Red starfish *Henricia sanguinolenta eschrichtii*
                               5. Toopook, one of the sculpins
                               6. Aghnoghook *Fucus sp*.
                               7. Opa, sea squirt
                               8. Makeetluk: Wolffish *Anarichus lupus*
                               9. Wapacha, see glossary

CHAPTER XXV   1. Tufted puffins *Lunda cirrhata*
                               2. Crested auklet *Aethia cristatella*

CHAPTER XXVI   1. Ivokiameet, people from the walrus place

CHAPTER XXIX   1. Phalaropes: Red phalarope *Phalaropus fulicarius*

CHAPTER XXX   1. Eiders: The common species on Sevuokuk is
                                  Pacific Eider *Somateria v. nigra*

GLOSSARY

THE CHARACTERS:

Anatoonga *Ana-toong-ga*
Apangalook *Ah-pahng-ah-look*
Asha *Ah-sha*
Assoonga *Ah-soong-ga*
Ega *E-ga*
Ikmallowa *Ik-mah-lo-wah*
Iyakatan *I-yak-a-tan*
Irrigoo *Ir-ri-goo*
Kaka *Ka-ka*
Kastevik *Kas-te-vik*
Kofkok *Kof-kok*
Kotwowin *Kot-wow-in*
Koonooku *Koo-noo-koo*
Kulukhon *Ku-lu-khon*
Lozama *Lo-zah-ma*
Massiu *Mas-si-u*
Mohok *Mo-hok*

Notangi *No-tang-gi*
Okoma *O-ko-ma*
Okohoni *O-ko-ho-ni*
Ozook *O-zook*
Pungwi *Pung-wie*
Rohltungu *Rohl-toong-gu*
Sekwo *Sek-wo*
Tatoowi *Ta-too-wi*
Timkaroo *Tim-kar-roo*
Tokoya *To-koy-a*
Tongyan *Tong-gy-yan*
Toozak *Too-zahk*
Walanga *Wa-lang-ga*
Walla *Wah-la*
Wohtillin *Woh-till-in*
Yahoh *Ya-hoh*
Yokho *Yok-ho*

THE MOONS:

Kan-ah-yung-a-si *(December)* *Moon of frost forming under the roof, very cold.*
Kah-loo-vik *(January)* *Moon for getting tom-cod with the throwing net.*
  The word means "net."
Nahze-ghoh-sek *(February)* *Moon of the approaching of young seal.*
Ta-heg-lokh-sek *(March)* *Moon of appearing of young big seal, Mukluk.*
Hogh-vek *(April)* *Moon for using bird slings, bolas.*
Keg-um-ah-na *(May)* *Summer-woman moon, spring.*
Pen-ah-vek *(June)* *Moon when the rivers begin to flow.*
Angot-ah-vek *(July)* *Moon of the flowering time of plants.*
Pal-eh-vek *(August)* *Moon of withering time of plants.*
Kom-la-vek *(September)* *Moon of freezing.*
A-ko-mak *(November)* *Moon of sitting, probably so called because it is the*
  slack season of little to do, after the fall storms and before the coming of the ice.

225

AND THE OTHER WORDS:

Ah-h   *Yes.*
Ahrola   *Ah-ro-lah, the dance.*
Aghvook   *Agh-vook, the whale. Used only of bowhead whale.*
Agnaya   *Ahg-nay-ah, the walrus woman in Ikmallowa's story.*
Agra   *Inner room of the ningloo.*
Aneelgulgit   *Ah-neel-gool-git, the perpetual snowdrifts at the western base*
   of the mountains which are along the southern part of the Island.
Ahalik   *Ah-hah-lik, the old-squaw duck,* Clangula hyemalis.
Anneepa   *Ah-nee-pa, the snowy owl,* Nyctea nyctea.
Apayapyeek   *Ah-pah-yap-yeek, Spider.*

Baleen   *Whalebone (not an Eskimo word however).*

Ievoghiyogameet   *I-eh-vog-i-yog-a-meet, one of the old villages at the*
   foot of the Cape Mountain at Sevuokuk. The word means "many walrus place."
   Suffix "meet" means "people from."
Inuit   *In-oo-eet, literally, "The People." This is the Eskimos'*
   name for themselves.
Iviek   *I-vi-yek, the walrus.*

Kalevak   *Ka-lee-vak, small under-pants of soft sealskin, worn by Eskimo women.*
Kayak   *Ki-yak, small decked-over skin boat. Used in early times on*
   Sevuokuk probably, but not in memory of present people. Toy kayaks were
   excavated from the lower levels of Kukulik mound.
Kehh   *Keh-h, exclamation of displeasure.*
Keyaghunuk   *Kee-ahg-gu-nuk, the greatest of all the spirits; the one*
   who sends the whales.
Kialegak   *Ki-a-li-gak, the southwest cape of the Island.*
Klooyak   *Kloo-yak, the Asiatic gyrfalcon,* Falco rusticolus uralensis.
   For some reason which we have not been able to determine, these white
   birds are sacred and inviolate among the Eskimos.
Kovvepek   *Ko-veh-pek, red fox.*
Kukulik   *Koo-koo-lik, the village on the northeast shore of Sevuokuk. Uninhabited*
   since the famine of 1878. The scene of archeological excavations in recent years.

Laluremka *Lah-loo-rem-kah, white man.*

Makeetluk *Mah-keet-luk, the wolf fish,* Anarichus lupus.
Mangona *Mahn-go-na, walrus skin with a layer of blubber attached.*
Mioghokmeet *Mee-o-gok-meet, one of the old villages near the foot of
    the Cape Mountain. Word means "the climbing place" (along the hillside).*
Miyowaghameet *Mee-o-wah-gah-meet, another old village near the mountain.*
Mukluk *Muk-luk, general term for the bearded seal,* Erignathus barbatus.
Munktuk *Munk-took, whale skin with layer of blubber attached.
    The greatest delicacy. It has a very mild flavor. That from the small
    beluga whale tastes like very mild kippered salmon, while that from
    the larger whales has a flavor like hazel nuts.*

Nanook *Na-nook, the polar bear, he who is considered to have human intelligence.*
Ngelkuk *Ngel-kook, the pelagic cormorant,* Phalacrocorax pelagicus.
Ningloo *Ning-gloo, the old time subterranean house, the kind used on
    the island until after the famine. No doubt the same word as igloo in other dialects,
    but this is the word used on Sevuokuk.*
Noghsuk *Noh-suk, general term for seal, any kind. It is hard to determine
    whether the last syllable is 'suk' or 'sek', it sounds somewhere between.*
Nughsopek *Noo-so-pek (or puk), large seal, usually meaning the mukluk.*
Nuna *Noo-nah, the ground, tundra.*
Nunivak *Noo-nee-vahk, plant or plants from which sour greens are made.
    Term also used for plants eaten fresh as greens. The most important
    one, that used for sour greens for winter, is* Sedum roseum *(L.) Scop.*

Ongtopuk *Ong-to-puk, big male walrus.*
Oolak *Oo-lahk, woman's knife. A half-circle shaped piece of stone (or, recently,
    steel or iron) set into a roughly half-circle shaped piece of wood,
    somewhat similar to our old-fashioned chopping knife. The women
    still prefer them to our scissors, even for cutting cloth or skins.*
Opa *O-pah, any of several forms of Ascidians, (sea squirts). The one with a
    stem or stalk is* Boltnia ovifera *(Linnaeus 1867). Another kind is* Ealocynthis
    aurantium *(Pallas 1787). Only the inside is eaten, after the salt water is squeezed out.
    The Eskimo bites the tough outer skin open and sucks out the soft inside.*

Poke   *Poke, a whole sealskin, from a seal skinned through the mouth, with all the openings plugged with stoppers made of ivory or wood or both, either used as a bag or inflated for use as a float in whaling or sealing. This is probably not an Eskimo word, but an adaptation of our word.*

Powooiliak   *Po-woo-il-i-ak, the southwest cape of the Island, the place discovered by Toozak.*

Powukpuk   *Pow-wuk-puk, meaning, in general, big mountain, but used particularly as the name of an outstanding volcanic peak on the east side of the Island.*

Sevuokuk   *Seh-voo-o-kuk, St. Lawrence Island.*

Sikkik   *Sik-kik, ground squirrel,* Citellus lyratus.

Siko   *See-ko, the ice, meaning the pack ice.*

Silimoka   *Sil-i-moka, general term for mushroom.*

Toopook   *Too-pook, one of the sculpins. There are many varieties in the region.*

Topek   *To-pek, summer tent made of walrus or other skins.*

Tukka, tukka   *Tukka, tukka, "Here, here." The term is used in the ball games and in calling dogs, and is difficult to define exactly.*

Ungiak   *Oong-i-ahk, skin boat. This is the Sevuokuk pronunciation. Other tribes call it oomiak.*

Ungiakpuk   *Oong-i-ahk-puk, the large skin boat.*

Wapacha   *Wah-pah-cha, the poisonous mushroom,* Amanita muscaria *Fr., called Wapacha when dried and used for dream purposes, called silimoka when fresh.*

Text type set by Interface California Corporation, Eureka, California
Display type set by Paul O. Giesey/Adcrafters, Portland, Oregon
Printing and Binding by Graphic Arts Center, Portland, Oregon